11+ Verbal Reasoning

Method, Technique and Practice

Madeline, Natasha & Stephanie Guyon

July 2009

ISBN 978-0-9556590-5-8

Published by PHI Education
15, Pimms Grove, High Wycombe, Buckinghamshire, HP13 7EE

Verbal Reasoning – Method, Technique & Practice
Contents

'Move a Letter'

What do they look like?...

In these questions, **one letter** can be moved from the first word to the second word, thereby making **two new words.**
The order of the other letters must not be changed and both new words must be correctly spelt.
Find the letter that moves and mark it on your answer sheet.

pride   hone

Multiple Choice Answer Box

p ☐
r ☐
i ☐
d ☐
e ☐

How to set about answering them...

Here you must change the two given words into two different, correctly spelt words by removing one letter from the first word and putting it into the second word.

Sometimes your first glance at the two words will tell you which letter you can move and therefore the one to mark on the answer sheet. If you cannot see the answer immediately in this way, then you need to try each letter in turn.

Take the first letter of the word on the left. If you were to remove it from the first word, would it then leave behind a correctly spelt word ? If not, try the next letter. If when you remove this letter you find that it does leave a correctly spelt word, try to fit this letter into the word on the right.

Try this letter at the beginning, end and between each letter of the word on the right. If that doesn't work you need to go back to the first word and try the next letter in the same way.

If after trying all of the letters in the first word you still cannot find the answer, then make a sensible guess.

Tips...

Make sure that the word on the left would become another properly spelt word without the letter that you've picked. It's very easy to just think about the word on the right and forget all about what happens to the one on the left.

Remember that if the word on the left has only one vowel, then this is not a good guess, as you cannot remove the vowel from a word with only one vowel, and leave a correctly spelt word behind.

'Move a Letter' – Worked Example

The Question……   The Answer Box……

below   **sat**

STEP 1

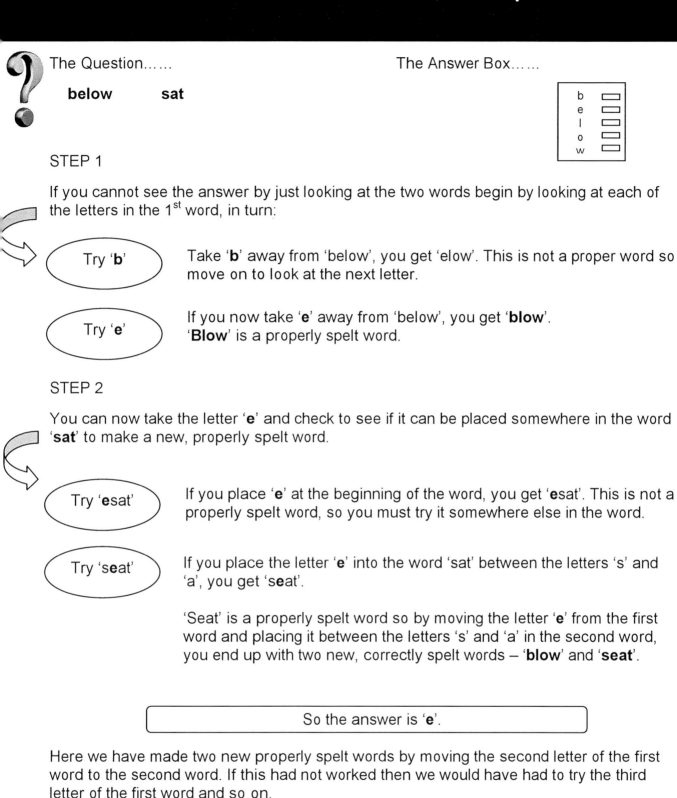

If you cannot see the answer by just looking at the two words begin by looking at each of the letters in the 1st word, in turn:

Try '**b**'   Take '**b**' away from 'below', you get 'elow'. This is not a proper word so move on to look at the next letter.

Try '**e**'   If you now take '**e**' away from 'below', you get '**blow**'. '**Blow**' is a properly spelt word.

STEP 2

You can now take the letter '**e**' and check to see if it can be placed somewhere in the word '**sat**' to make a new, properly spelt word.

Try '**esat**'   If you place '**e**' at the beginning of the word, you get '**e**sat'. This is not a properly spelt word, so you must try it somewhere else in the word.

Try '**seat**'   If you place the letter '**e**' into the word 'sat' between the letters 's' and 'a', you get '**s**eat'.

'Seat' is a properly spelt word so by moving the letter '**e**' from the first word and placing it between the letters 's' and 'a' in the second word, you end up with two new, correctly spelt words – '**blow**' and '**seat**'.

So the answer is '**e**'.

Here we have made two new properly spelt words by moving the second letter of the first word to the second word. If this had not worked then we would have had to try the third letter of the first word and so on.

 Mark the multiple choice answer box as shown ⟹

'Move a Letter' – Example Questions

In these questions, **one letter** can be moved from the first word to the second word, thereby making **two new words.**

The order of the other letters must not be changed and both new words must be correctly spelt.

Find the letter that moves and mark it on your answer sheet.

Example   Answer

    pride   hone   **p** (the two new words are **ride** and **phone**)

QUESTION 1

slide   spice

1.
s	▭
l	▭
i	▭
d	▭
e	▭

QUESTION 2

theme   swat

2.
t	▭
h	▭
e	▭
m	▭
e	▭

QUESTION 3

plane   mode

3.
p	▭
l	▭
a	▭
n	▭
e	▭

QUESTION 4

furry   camp

4.
f	▭
u	▭
r	▭
r	▭
y	▭

QUESTION 5

going   pant

5.
g	▭
o	▭
i	▭
n	▭
g	▭

QUESTION 6

heart   spout

6.

h	☐
e	☐
a	☐
r	☐
t	☐

QUESTION 7

rodeo   live

7.

r	☐
o	☐
d	☐
e	☐
o	☐

QUESTION 8

taken   early

8.

t	☐
a	☐
k	☐
e	☐
n	☐

QUESTION 9

beast   peak

9.

b	☐
e	☐
a	☐
s	☐
t	☐

QUESTION 10

solid   plot

10.

s	☐
o	☐
l	☐
i	☐
d	☐

QUESTION 11

those   closes

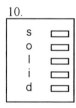

11.

t	☐
h	☐
o	☐
s	☐
e	☐

QUESTION 12

solve   duet

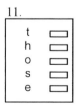

12.

s	☐
o	☐
l	☐
v	☐
e	☐

'Missing Letter'

What do they look like?...

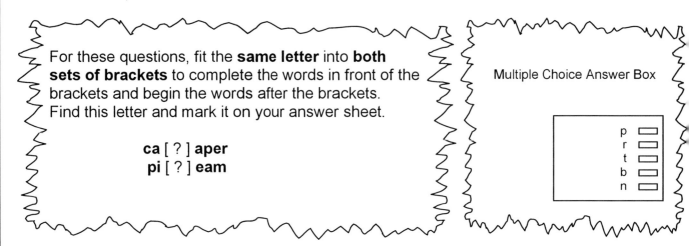

For these questions, fit the **same letter** into **both sets of brackets** to complete the words in front of the brackets and begin the words after the brackets. Find this letter and mark it on your answer sheet.

ca [?] aper
pi [?] eam

Multiple Choice Answer Box

p ☐
r ☐
t ☐
b ☐
n ☐

How to set about answering them...

The multiple choice answer box will suggest a number of letters for you to try in place of the question marks [?]. **Only one** of these letters will be able to fit into **both sets of brackets** to complete the words in front of the brackets and begin the words after the brackets. **The same letter must be used in both brackets** and all four words must be correctly spelt, proper words.

Take a quick look at the four incomplete words and the options given in the multiple choice. Sometimes you may be lucky and immediately spot the letter that will complete <u>all four</u> words.

Can't find the answer ?

Take the first letter from the multiple choice options. Try it in the brackets. Does it complete not just one or two or three of the words, but all four ?

If not, try the second letter. Again, can it complete the <u>four</u> words ? If not, it will not do !

Continue until you have found the letter that completes <u>all four</u> words.

Tips...

If you very quickly find a letter that works in both brackets, quickly check the remaining letters to confirm that none of them also appears to work with all four words. Remember, only ONE of the suggested letters will work with all four words.

If none of the letters seems to fit with all four words, decide which ones are definitely wrong and then choose the most likely from the remaining letters.

'Missing Letter' - Worked Example

The question......   The Answer box......

mea [?] oble
pi [?] ew

STEP 1

Take each letter from the answer box in turn.

Try '**r**') **mea [r] oble**   'mear' ?, 'roble' ?, 'pir' ?, rew' ?
           pi [r] ew   <u>None</u> of these words look right.

Try '**t**') **mea [t] oble**   'meat'... looks OK, 'pit'... looks OK
           pi [t] ew   **BUT**
                                'toble' ? , 'tew' ?
                            Neither of these words looks right.

Try '**n**') **mea [n] oble**   'mean'... looks OK, 'noble'.... looks OK,
           pi [n] ew   'pin'.... looks OK, 'new'.... looks OK

So it looks likely that the correct answer is '**n**'.

STEP 2

Quickly check out the remaining two letters.....

Try '**l**') **mea [l] oble**   'loble' ?, 'pil' ? , 'lew' ?
           pi [l] ew   None of these words look right.

Try '**d**') **mea [d] oble**   'doble ? 'pid' ?
           pi [d] ew   Neither of these words looks right.

So the answer in '**n**'

Mark the multiple choice answer box as shown. $\Longrightarrow$

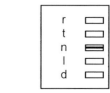

'Missing letter' – Example Questions

For these questions, fit the **same letter** into **both sets of brackets** to complete the words in front of the brackets and begin the words after the brackets.
Find this letter and mark it on your answer sheet.

Example

ca [?] aper
pi [?] eam

Answer

'**t**' (the four words are **cat, taper, pit, team**)

QUESTION 1

plum [?] ound
cra [?] ite

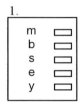

QUESTION 2

comm [?] mple
delt [?] steroid

QUESTION 3

war [?] usk
swor [?] ame

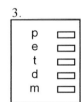

QUESTION 4

swin [?] rapple
bra [?] nome

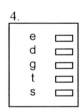

QUESTION 5

wor [?] ase
agre [?] ither

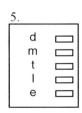

'Missing letter' – Example Questions

QUESTION 6

sta [?] elate
cleane [?] ambler

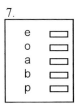

QUESTION 7

lim [?] allet
plum [?] roud

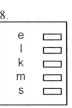

QUESTION 8

stal [?] ack
hoste [?] itre

QUESTION 9

bal [?] aze
sai [?] ental

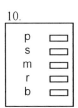

QUESTION 10

clas [?] ink
dee [?] olar

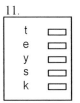

QUESTION 11

bas [?] ew
mas [?] ale

QUESTION 12

for [?] ill
pel [?] own

'Closest in Meaning'

What do they look like?...

For these questions, find **two words**, one from each group, that are **closest in meaning**.
Mark both of these words on your answer sheet.

(congested   vacant   spacious)
(indigestion   crowded   area)

Multiple Choice Answer Box

congested ▭	indigestion ▭
vacant ▭	crowded ▭
spacious ▭	area ▭

How to set about answering them...

Read the six words in the two brackets. You need to match one word from the first bracket with one word from the second bracket.

You may immediately see the pair which go together because they are the CLOSEST in meaning. If you do, mark these two words on the multiple choice answer sheet and move onto the next question.

If you don't see the answer immediately, take the first word from the first bracket and try it out with the three words in the second bracket in turn. No match ?

Try the second word from the first bracket and try it out with the three words in the second bracket in turn. Still no match ?

Finally try the third word from the first bracket and try it out with the three words in the second bracket in turn.

Tips...

Write a big letter 'C' next to the question on your question paper and underline the word 'Closest' in the question to remind yourself that you are looking for two words that are closest in meaning. It's very easy to accidentally pick two words that are opposite in meaning if you do not do this.

The Question......

(button   pull   boat)
(rope   tug   push)

The Answer Box......

button ▭		rope ▭
pull ▭		tug ▭
boat ▭		push ▭

STEP 1

Take the first word from the first bracket and the first word from the second bracket:-

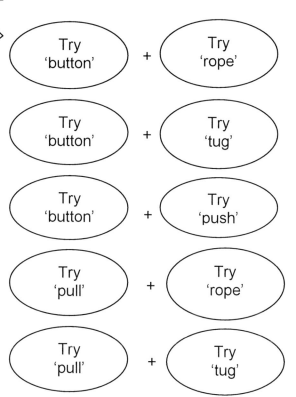

These are not close in meaning so now, take the first word from the first bracket and the second word from the second bracket.

These are not close in meaning either so now take the first word from the first bracket and the third word from the second bracket.

These are not close in meaning either so move on to the second word from the first bracket and the first word from the second bracket.

These are not close in meaning either so take the second word from the first bracket and the second word from the second bracket.

'Pull' and 'tug' have the same meaning.

STEP 2

Check to make sure that the remaining options don't also appear to have a similar meaning. If so, then you need to decide which are the best two for your answer.

So the answer is '**pull**' and '**tug**'.

Mark the multiple choice answer box as shown ⟹

button ▭		rope ▭
pull ▬		tug ▬
boat ▭		push ▭

For these questions, find **two words**, one from each group, that are **closest in meaning**.
Mark both of these words on your answer sheet.

Example

(congested   vacant   spacious)
(indigestion   crowded   area)

Answer

congested   crowded

QUESTION 1

(good   likeable   friend)
(popular   unpleasant   relative)

1.

good ☐	popular ☐
likeable ☐	unpleasant ☐
friend ☐	relative ☐

QUESTION 2

(tune   chord   lyrics)
(sing   choir   melody)

2.

tune ☐	sing ☐
chord ☐	choir ☐
lyrics ☐	melody ☐

QUESTION 3

(good   sweets   favourite)
(preferred   sport   like)

3.

good ☐	preferred ☐
sweets ☐	sport ☐
favourite ☐	like ☐

QUESTION 4

(tranquil   rest   sleep)
(silence   calm   dampen)

4.

tranquil ☐	silence ☐
rest ☐	calm ☐
sleep ☐	dampen ☐

QUESTION 5

(pressurise   suppress   pump)
(valve   tyre   subdue)

5.

pressurise ☐	valve ☐
suppress ☐	tyre ☐
pump ☐	subdue ☐

QUESTION 6

(ruler   curve   rule)
(line   govern   straight)

6.

ruler ☐	line ☐
curve ☐	govern ☐
rule ☐	straight ☐

QUESTION 7

(sharp   edge   area)
(periphery   blunt   blade)

7.

sharp ☐	periphery ☐
edge ☐	blunt ☐
area ☐	blade ☐

QUESTION 8

(revolve   recoil   steady)
(turn   pistol   shoot)

8.

revolve ☐	turn ☐
recoil ☐	pistol ☐
steady ☐	shoot ☐

QUESTION 9

(question   revolution   assessment)
(judge   evaluation   evolution)

9.

question ☐	judge ☐
revolution ☐	evaluation ☐
assessment ☐	evolution ☐

QUESTION 10

(fascinating   curiosity   scrutinise)
(disinterest   interest   ignore)

10.

fascinating ☐	disinterest ☐
curiosity ☐	interest ☐
scrutinise ☐	ignore ☐

QUESTION 11

(bandage   discomfort   injury)
(pain   anaesthetic   wound)

11.

bandage ☐	pain ☐
discomfort ☐	anaesthetic ☐
injury ☐	wound ☐

QUESTION 12

(enchanting   enliven   incarcerate)
(captivating   repeat   criticise)

12.

enchanting ☐	captivating ☐
enliven ☐	repeat ☐
incarcerate ☐	criticise ☐

'Missing Three-Letter Word'

What do they look like?...

In these sentences, **three consecutive letters** have been taken out of the word in capitals.
These three letters spell a proper word without changing their order.
The sentence that you make must make sense.
Mark the correct three-letter word on your answer sheet.

The class was asked to **CRE** its own story.

Multiple Choice Answer Box

RAY	☐
EAT	☐
SAY	☐
ORE	☐
SHE	☐

How to set about answering them...

First read the sentence and think about its meaning. This may give you a clue about the letters in bold type which need to have a three-letter word added to them in order to make the sentence make complete sense.

If you think you now know what the complete word should be, write the completed word you are thinking of over the letters in bold on the question sheet.

Now cross out the same letters that have been given in bold from your word. You may now have one of the three-letter words on the multiple choice answer sheet. If so, mark this word on your answer sheet.

If you cannot find the answer, look carefully now at the five options in the multiple choice. Try to fit the first three-letter word into the group of bold letters. You cannot separate or rearrange the order of the three letters.

Are you able to fit the three-letter word anywhere within the group of bold letters to make a correctly spelt word ?

If not, try the next three-letter word. Could it fit anywhere within the group of bold letters to make a correctly spelt word ?

Keep moving though the five options until you have found the answer.

Tips...

Once you think you've found the correct three-letter word to make a correctly spelt word, make sure that the word you've made makes sense within the sentence.

'Missing Three-Letter Word' – Worked Example

 The Question……

The Answer Box……

He **SPED** on the wet floor.

```
LIP  ▭
LAP  ▭
LID  ▭
POW  ▭
LOP  ▭
```

STEP 1

Read the sentence and if you can't immediately think of the missing word, begin to try each of the options in turn.

 Take the first three-letter word provided in the answer box, 'LIP', and try to fit it in or around the group of bold letters.

Try 'LIP **SPED**'   No, that doesn't make a proper word.

Try '**S** LIP **PED**'   'SLIPPED' is a proper word and the sentence 'He SLIPPED on the wet floor.' makes sense.

STEP 2

 Check through the other combinations to make sure that there are no other proper words that make sense in the given sentence.

Try 'LAP **SPED**'   No, that doesn't make a proper word.

Try '**S** LAP **PED**'   'SLAPPED' is a proper word but the sentence 'He slapped on the wet floor.' does not make sense.

Continue checking through the options to make sure that you have chosen the best answer.

So the answer is '**LIP**'.

 Mark the multiple choice answer box as shown
```
LIP  ▤
LAP  ▭
LID  ▭
POW  ▭
LOP  ▭
```

'Missing Three-Letter Word' – Example Questions

In these sentences, **three consecutive letters** have been taken out of the word in capitals.
These three letters spell a proper word without changing their order.
The sentence that you make must make sense.
Mark the correct three-letter word on your answer sheet.

Example   Answer

The rides at the **FGROUND** were breathtaking.   **AIR**   (the completed word is **FAIRGROUND**)

QUESTION 1

HSTY is the best policy.

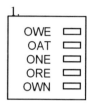

1.
OWE ☐
OAT ☐
ONE ☐
ORE ☐
OWN ☐

QUESTION 2

The prisoners planned their **ESE**.

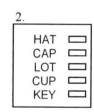

2.
HAT ☐
CAP ☐
LOT ☐
CUP ☐
KEY ☐

QUESTION 3

The injured athlete was unable to **COMPE** the race.

3.
PET ☐
PAT ☐
PEA ☐
LET ☐
SUM ☐

QUESTION 4

The computer's battery was running low on **PR**.

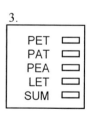

4.
OUR ☐
ORE ☐
ARE ☐
PAR ☐
OWE ☐

QUESTION 5

Chew your food well before you **SWOW**.

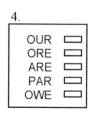

5.
ALE ☐
OIL ☐
ALL ☐
AWL ☐
EAR ☐

'Missing Three-Letter Word' - Example Questions

QUESTION 6

The horse's **SLE** was old and worn.

6.

EAR	☐
ARE	☐
LET	☐
ADD	☐
LOT	☐

QUESTION 7

Walking quickly made him **SW**.

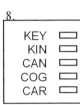

7.

ARE	☐
ATE	☐
EVE	☐
ORE	☐
EAT	☐

QUESTION 8

After the hurricane, it was hard to **RENIZE** the place.

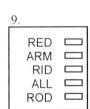

8.

KEY	☐
KIN	☐
CAN	☐
COG	☐
CAR	☐

QUESTION 9

It was difficult to **PICT** his next move.

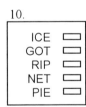

9.

RED	☐
ARM	☐
RID	☐
ALL	☐
ROD	☐

QUESTION 10

The **MAG** strutted about noisily on the tin roof.

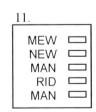

10.

ICE	☐
GOT	☐
RIP	☐
NET	☐
PIE	☐

QUESTION 11

James was always first to hand in his **HOORK**.

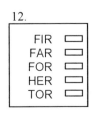

11.

MEW	☐
NEW	☐
MAN	☐
RID	☐
MAN	☐

QUESTION 12

Please mind the gap between the train and the **PLATM**.

12.

FIR	☐
FAR	☐
FOR	☐
HER	☐
TOR	☐

What do they look like?...

For these questions, find the two words, **one from each set of brackets,** that will complete the statement in the best way.
Mark both words on your answer sheet.

Fish is to
(chips   scales   cod)
as **bird** is to
(feathers   nest   wing).

Multiple Choice Answer Box

chips ☐   feathers ☐
scales ☐   nest ☐
cod ☐   wing ☐

How to set about answering them...

With this type of question you need to complete the sentence to make an analogy.

You need to look at the first keyword of the sentence ('**Fish**') and link it to one of the words in the brackets that follows it and then using the same association link the second keyword ('**bird**') to a word from the second set of brackets.

In the example you see that fish can be linked to scales in the same way as '**bird**' can be linked to '**feathers**'.

Although each of the keywords can be linked in some way with all three of the words contained in the following brackets, only scales and feathers have the same association – i.e. a fish is covered in scales and a bird is covered in feathers.

Whilst '**Fish**' can be linked to '**cod**' or '**chips**', there is no similar association for '**bird**' and the three words in the bracket that follows it :-

Cod is a type of fish but you could not say that '**feathers**', '**nest**' or '**wing**' are a type of bird.

Chips can be eaten with a fish but you could not say that '**feathers**', '**nest**' or '**wing**' could be eaten with a bird.

Tips...

Make sure you are clear about the relationship between each pair of words. The relationship between the first two words <u>must</u> be the same as the relationship between the second two words.

'Word Associations' – Worked Example

The Question……

Heart is to
(blood   love   centre)
as **perimeter** is to
(veins   edge   road)

The Answer Box……

blood ▢	veins ▢
love ▢	edge ▢
centre ▢	road ▢

STEP 1

Look at the associations between each of the words in the first bracket (blood, love and centre) and the first keyword (Heart) and then see if a **similar association** exists between the words in the second bracket and the second keyword :

Try 'blood'   Blood is pumped by a heart but you **could not** say that '**veins**', '**edge**' or 'road' had any **similar association** with the word 'perimeter'.

STEP 2

Try 'love'   Love is an emotion associated with the heart, but you **could not** say that '**veins**', '**edge**' or '**road**' had any **similar association** with the word '**perimeter**'.

STEP 3

Try 'centre'   Centre is another word for the middle or the '**heart**' of something, for example 'the heart of the city' is the centre of the city. A **similar association could** be made here between 'perimeter' and the word 'edge'. If '**heart**' can mean the '**centre**' of something, and '**perimeter**' means the '**edge**' of something' then a common relationship exists.

So the answer is **'Heart is to centre as perimeter is to edge.'**

Mark the multiple choice answer box as shown ⟹

blood ▢	veins ▢
love ▢	edge ▣
centre ▣	road ▢

For these questions, find the two words, **one from each set of brackets,** that will complete the statement in the best way.
Mark both words on your answer sheet.

Example   Answer

Fish is to   **scales, feathers**
(chips   scales   cod)
as **bird** is to
(feathers   nest   wing).

QUESTION 1

Car is to
(drive   road   petrol)
as **train** is to
(track   practice   passengers).

1.
drive ▭	track ▭
road ▭	practice ▭
petrol ▭	passengers ▭

QUESTION 2

Kilogram is to
(wait   sugar   weight)
as **litre** is to
(area   volume   length).

2.
wait ▭	area ▭
sugar ▭	volume ▭
weight ▭	length ▭

QUESTION 3

Smart is to
(trams   card   clever)
as **madam** is to
(master   madam   lady).

3.
trams ▭	master ▭
card ▭	madam ▭
clever ▭	lady ▭

QUESTION 4

Divide is to
(arithmetic   dissect   subtract)
as **multiply** is to
(calculate   add   logarithm).

4.
arithmetic ▭	calculate ▭
dissect ▭	add ▭
subtract ▭	logarithm ▭

QUESTION 5

Tight is to
(rope   loose   lose)
as **slack** is to
(taut   string   spare).

5.
rope ▭	taut ▭
loose ▭	string ▭
lose ▭	spare ▭

QUESTION 6

Bind is to
(book   find   tie)
as **bound** is to
(novel   heading   found).

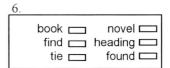

6.

book ▢	novel ▢
find ▢	heading ▢
tie ▢	found ▢

QUESTION 7

Slide is to
(glide   park   slid)
as **run** is to
(race   ran   ink).

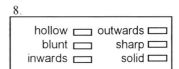

7.

glide ▢	race ▢
park ▢	ran ▢
slid ▢	ink ▢

QUESTION 8

Concave is to
(hollow   blunt   inwards)
as **convex** is to
(outwards   sharp   solid).

8.

hollow ▢	outwards ▢
blunt ▢	sharp ▢
inwards ▢	solid ▢

QUESTION 9

Propeller is to
(rotate   propel   boat)
as **rudder** is to
(steer   ship   sail).

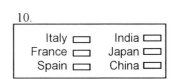

9.

rotate ▢	steer ▢
propel ▢	ship ▢
boat ▢	sail ▢

QUESTION 10

Paris is to
(Italy   France   Spain)
as **Tokyo** is to
(India   Japan   China).

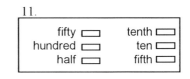

10.

Italy ▢	India ▢
France ▢	Japan ▢
Spain ▢	China ▢

QUESTION 11

Ten is to
(fifty   hundred   half)
as **one** is to
(tenth   ten   fifth).

11.

fifty ▢	tenth ▢
hundred ▢	ten ▢
half ▢	fifth ▢

QUESTION 12

Bass is to
(fish   drum   low)
as **treble** is to
(high   clef   meat).

12.

fish ▢	high ▢
drum ▢	clef ▢
low ▢	meat ▢

'Opposite in Meaning'

What do they look like?...

Below are two groups of words.
Choose **two words**, one from each group, that are most **opposite** in meaning.
Mark the two words on your answer sheet.

(formal   accident   dinner)
(official   casual   dress)

Multiple Choice Answer Box

formal ▭	official ▭
accident ▭	casual ▭
dinner ▭	dress ▭

How to set about answering them...

In these questions you have <u>two</u> groups of <u>three</u> words.

You need to match one word from the first group with one from the second group, that are most opposite in meaning.

The layout of the question is the same as for the 'closest in meaning' questions so be careful not to confuse them !

One way to remind yourself that you are looking for opposites and not the 'closest in meaning' is to underline the word 'opposite' in the question and to write the letters '**OPP**' at the side of the question sheet.

If you do not immediately see the answer, try taking each of the three words in the first group in turn. Does the first word of the first group have a word in the second group that could be its opposite ? If not, try the second word. Does the second word from the first group have a word in the second group that could be its opposite ? If not, try the third word from the first group. Does this have a word in the second group that could be its opposite ?

Tips...

It is very easy to accidentally pick two words that are closest in meaning.

Write the letters '**OPP**' next to the questions and underline the word 'opposite' in the question to remind you that you are looking for the two words which are <u>opposite</u> in meaning.

'Opposite in Meaning' – Worked Example

The Question......

(garden   in   shop)
(up   hotel   out)

The Answer Box......

garden ▭	up ▭
in ▭	hotel ▭
shop ▭	out ▭

STEP 1

Write 'OPP' on the question sheet and underline the word 'opposite' in the question.

STEP 2

Take the first word from the first bracket (garden) and try it alongside each of the three words from the second bracket to see if it has an opposite.

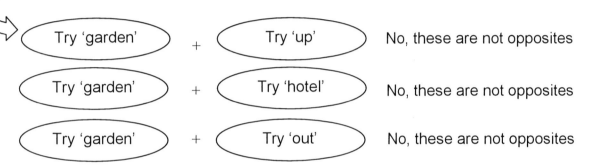

Try 'garden'   +   Try 'up'   No, these are not opposites

Try 'garden'   +   Try 'hotel'   No, these are not opposites

Try 'garden'   +   Try 'out'   No, these are not opposites

STEP 2

Now take the second word from the first bracket and try it alongside each of the three words from the second bracket to see if it has an opposite.

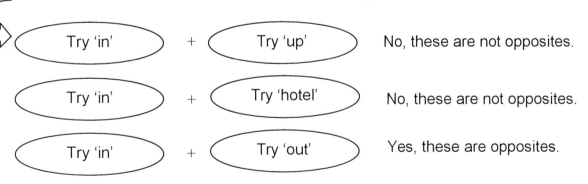

Try 'in'   +   Try 'up'   No, these are not opposites.

Try 'in'   +   Try 'hotel'   No, these are not opposites.

Try 'in'   +   Try 'out'   Yes, these are opposites.

So the answer is 'in' and 'out'.

Mark the multiple choice answer box as shown   ⟹

garden ▭	up ▭
in ▣	hotel ▭
shop ▭	out ▣

'Opposite in Meaning' – Example Questions

Below are two groups of words. Choose **two words**, one from each group, that are most **opposite** in meaning.
Mark the two words on your answer sheet.

Example   Answer

    (formal   accident   dinner)   **formal   casual**
    (official   casual   dress)

QUESTION 1

    (snail   race   fast)
    (quick   slow   shell)

1.

snail ☐	quick ☐
race ☐	slow ☐
fast ☐	shell ☐

QUESTION 2

    (wealth   cash   hardship)
    (money   beggar   poverty)

2.

wealth ☐	money ☐
cash ☐	beggar ☐
hardship ☐	poverty ☐

QUESTION 3

    (demolish   sturdy   security)
    (solid   rickety   house)

3.

demolish ☐	solid ☐
sturdy ☐	rickety ☐
security ☐	house ☐

QUESTION 4

    (kitchen   float   water)
    (carnival   sink   swim)

4.

kitchen ☐	carnival ☐
float ☐	sink ☐
water ☐	swim ☐

QUESTION 5

    (vast   hour   spectacular)
    (minute   clock   enormous)

5.

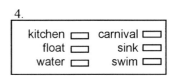

vast ☐	minute ☐
hour ☐	clock ☐
spectacular ☐	enormous ☐

QUESTION 6

(crush   precis   extend)
(concierge   shorten   intend)

6.

crush ☐	concierge ☐
précis ☐	shorten ☐
extend ☐	intend ☐

QUESTION 7

(complex   dull   thrilling)
(yawn   boring   complain)

7.

complex ☐	yawn ☐
dull ☐	boring ☐
thrilling ☐	complain ☐

QUESTION 8

(attack   victory   defend)
(protest   win   defeat)

8.

attack ☐	protest ☐
victory ☐	win ☐
defend ☐	defeat ☐

QUESTION 9

(admire   retain   examine)
(detest   respect   detain)

9.

admire ☐	detest ☐
retain ☐	respect ☐
examine ☐	detain ☐

QUESTION 10

(thrifty   generous   savings)
(miserly   priceless   expensive)

10.

thrifty ☐	miserly ☐
generous ☐	priceless ☐
savings ☐	expensive ☐

QUESTION 11

(gradual   rude   cross)
(slowly   angry   abrupt)

11.

gradual ☐	slowly ☐
rude ☐	angry ☐
cross ☐	abrupt ☐

QUESTION 12

(cheat   justice   fair)
(unjust   light   incorrect)

12.

cheat ☐	unjust ☐
justice ☐	light ☐
fair ☐	incorrect ☐

What do they look like?...

In these sentences, a **four-letter** word is hidden between two words that are next to each other. Find the **two words** that contain the hidden word and mark them on your answer sheet.

Her friends all stayed for tea.

Multiple Choice Answer Box

Her friends ☐
friends all ☐
all stayed ☐
stayed for ☐
for tea. ☐

How to set about answering them...

Read over the sentence. The four-letter word may immediately show itself to you !

The four-letter word will always cross over <u>two</u> words and will be formed from some letters at the end of one word and some letters at the beginning of the next word.

If you can't immediately see the hidden four-letter word, try moving your two thumbs along the sentence. Put your thumbs to the left of the last three letters of the first word and your right thumb to the right of first letter of the second word. Does that make a word ?

If not, slide your left thumb one letter to the right so that you can see the last two letters of the first word and slide your right thumb to the right so that you can see the first two letters of the second word. Does that make a word ?

If not, move your thumbs again one letter to the right so that you can see the last letter of the first word and the first three letters of the second word. Does that make a word ?

If not, the hidden word must be between two other words. Move onto the second and third words in the sentence and, using your thumbs again, repeat the process.

Keep moving along each pair of words until you find the hidden word.

Tips...

It is usually quicker and easier to work directly on the multiple choice answer sheet.

'Hidden Four-Letter Word' – Worked Example

The Question……

'Drivers often exceed the speed limit.'

The Answer Box……

> Drivers often ☐
> often exceed ☐
> exceed the ☐
> the speed ☐
> speed limit. ☐

STEP 1

Take the first two words and using both of your thumbs, cover up all but the last three letters of the first word and all but the first letter of the second word.

Drivers often   'erso' is not a word so slide your thumbs one place to the right.

Drivers often   'rsof' is not a word either, so slide your thumbs along again

Drivers often   'soft' is a proper word and so mark the answer on the multiple choice answer sheet next to '**Drivers often**'

If you had not found a proper four-letter word when looking at the words 'Drivers' and 'often', you would then move on to the words 'often' and 'exceed' and repeat the process. You would carry on along the sentence until you find a properly spelt four-letter word.

> So the answer is '**Drivers often**'.

Mark the multiple choice answer box as shown ⟹

> Drivers often ▉
> often exceed ☐
> exceed the ☐
> the speed ☐
> speed limit. ☐

'Hidden Four-Letter Word' – Example Questions

In these sentences, a **four-letter** word is hidden between two words that are next to each other.

Find the **two words** that contain the hidden word and mark them on your answer sheet.

Example	Answer
Her friends all stayed for tea.	**for tea** (the hidden word is **fort**)

QUESTION 1

We said prayers in church today.

1.
We said	☐
said prayers	☐
prayers in	☐
in church	☐
church today.	☐

QUESTION 2

Photographers sometimes use wide angle lenses.

2.
Photographers sometimes	☐
sometimes use	☐
use wide	☐
wide angle	☐
angle lenses.	☐

QUESTION 3

The panda really liked his bamboo.

3.
The panda	☐
panda really	☐
really liked	☐
liked his	☐
his bamboo.	☐

QUESTION 4

Tom left his front door unlocked.

4.
Tom left	☐
left his	☐
his front	☐
front door	☐
door unlocked.	☐

QUESTION 5

George loved being left in charge.

5.
George loved	☐
loved being	☐
being left	☐
left in	☐
in charge.	☐

QUESTION 6

John is paid less than Peter.

6.

John is	▭
is paid	▭
paid less	▭
less than	▭
than Peter.	▭

QUESTION 7

Toto hid under the garden table.

7.

Toto hid	▭
hid under	▭
under the	▭
the garden	▭
garden table.	▭

QUESTION 8

We drove round in endless circles.

8.

We drove	▭
drove round	▭
round in	▭
in endless	▭
endless circles.	▭

QUESTION 9

The potholer longed to see daylight.

9.

The potholer	▭
potholer longed	▭
longed to	▭
to see	▭
see daylight.	▭

QUESTION 10

Finally, Philip earned the team's respect.

10.

Finally, Phillip	▭
Philip earned	▭
earned the	▭
the team's	▭
team's respect.	▭

QUESTION 11

Alex tried on his new shirt.

11.

Alex tried	▭
tried on	▭
on his	▭
his new	▭
new shirt.	▭

QUESTION 12

Shirley ate the hot noodles slowly.

12.

Shirley ate	▭
ate the	▭
the hot	▭
hot noodles	▭
noodles slowly.	▭

'Odd Two Out'

What do they look like?...

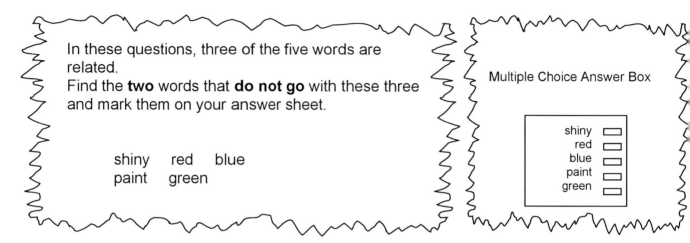

In these questions, three of the five words are related.
Find the **two** words that **do not go** with these three and mark them on your answer sheet.

shiny   red   blue
paint   green

Multiple Choice Answer Box

shiny ▭
red ▭
blue ▭
paint ▭
green ▭

How to set about answering them...

Read over the list of five words carefully. You need to remove two words from the list and leave behind three.

The three words which you leave behind go together and make a group.

The two words that you remove are the 'odd two out' and you need to mark both of these on the multiple choice answer sheet.

Think about any common groupings that the words could fit into. In this case, 'red', 'blue', and 'green' are all colours, whereas 'shiny' and 'paint' could not be described as colours and therefore do not fit into the same group as the others. This makes them the 'odd two out'.

Remember, the 'odd two out' do not need to have any connection with each other.

Tips...

Remember too that some words have more than one meaning or, as in the case of the worked example which follows, are close in terms of spelling to another word with a different meaning. Try to spot these when looking at the words in these questions.

The question……

**apex   peak   spy
peer   summit**

The Answer box……

apex	▭
peak	▭
spy	▭
peer	▭
summit	▭

STEP 1

Consider the meaning of each of the words... (you will need to do this in your head).

'apex'

An '**apex**' refers to the top of something.

'peak'

The '**peak**' of something is either the top of something or is the name given to the front of a cap or hat. But <u>don't confuse</u> it with the word 'peek' which means 'to look'.

'spy'

The word '**spy**' can be referring to a secret agent but it also means to 'look' or to 'see'. For example, 'I spy with my little eye'.

'peer'

The word '**peer**' means to look.

'summit'

The word '**summit**' is typically used to describe the top of a mountain.

STEP 2

Identify the similarities between each of the words...

The words '**apex**', '**peak**' and '**summit**' all mean '**top**', whilst '**spy**' and '**peer**' mean to '**look**'.

Clearly, knowing the different spellings and meanings of the words '**peak**' and '**peek**' is important in this question.

So the answer is '**spy**' and '**peer**'.

Mark the multiple choice answer box as shown.

apex	▭
peak	▭
spy	▣
peer	▣
summit	▭

'Odd Two Out' – Example Questions

In these questions, three of the five words are related.
Find the **two** words that **do not go** with these three and mark them on your answer sheet.

Example

    shiny   red   blue
    paint   green

Answer

shiny   paint

QUESTION 1

    daisy   petal   tulip
    stem   daffodil

1.
daisy	▭
petal	▭
tulip	▭
stem	▭
daffodil	▭

QUESTION 2

    tools   shed   hut
    shack   garden

2.
tools	▭
shed	▭
hut	▭
shack	▭
garden	▭

QUESTION 3

    gigantic   miniscule   huge
    vast   size

3.
gigantic	▭
miniscule	▭
huge	▭
vast	▭
size	▭

QUESTION 4

    protracted   ruler   extended
    long   geometry

4.
protracted	▭
ruler	▭
extended	▭
long	▭
geometry	▭

QUESTION 5

    tale   fable   story
    squirrel   end

5.
tale	▭
fable	▭
story	▭
squirrel	▭
end	▭

QUESTION 6

    shatter   brake   fracture
    fragment   leg

6.
shatter	▭
brake	▭
fracture	▭
fragment	▭
leg	▭

QUESTION 7

silent   quite   hushed
mute   noise

7.
silent ☐
quite ☐
hushed ☐
mute ☐
noise ☐

QUESTION 8

plane   coach   helicopter
glider   plain

8.
plane ☐
coach ☐
helicopter ☐
glider ☐
plain ☐

QUESTION 9

obtain   bye   purchase
acquire   farewell

9.
obtain ☐
bye ☐
purchase ☐
acquire ☐
farewell ☐

QUESTION 10

suspend   hang   picture
postpone   interrupt

10.
suspend ☐
hang ☐
picture ☐
postpone ☐
interrupt ☐

QUESTION 11

fruit   orange   chime
ring   peal

11.
fruit ☐
orange ☐
chime ☐
ring ☐
peal ☐

QUESTION 12

forego   surrender   army
soldier   sacrifice

12.
forego ☐
surrender ☐
army ☐
soldier ☐
sacrifice ☐

'Compound Words'

What do they look like?...

For these questions, join a word from the first group with a word from the second group to make a correctly spelt, new word. The word from the first group must always come first and the order of the letters must not be changed.

(cob   cup   cub)
(board   bored   led)

Multiple Choice Answer Box

cob ☐   board ☐
cup ☐   bored ☐
cub ☐   led ☐

How to set about answering them...

Here you need to make a compound word by joining one word from the first group with one from the second group.

First, glance across the two groups. You may immediately see which two words can be joined together to make a correctly spelt compound word. If so, mark these two words on your answer sheet.

If you did not see the answer immediately, take the first word from the first bracket. Will it join any of the words in the second bracket ?

Remember, the word from the first bracket must go first and that you must make a correctly spelt word.

If not, try the second word from the first bracket. Will that join any of the words in the second bracket ? Again, remember that the word from the first bracket must go first and that you must make a correctly spelt word.

Finally, try the third word from the first bracket. Will it join any of the words in the second group to make a correctly spelt word ?

If you are struggling with the question, it usually helps to write out the options you have just tried in your head. Often, when you see the two words written together, it is easier to see the answer.

Tips...

Writing the words down before you mark your answer sheet will help to check the spelling of the compound word.

'Compound Words' - Worked Example

 The Question......

(out   up   down)
(bite   like   law)

The Answer Box......

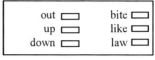

STEP 1

Look at the words in the two brackets: Can you immediately see the answer?...No?

STEP 2

Take the first word from the first bracket and put it with the first word from the second bracket to see if it makes a correctly spelt compound word:-

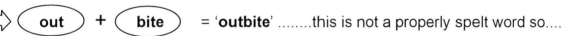

(out) + (bite)   = 'outbite' ....this is not a properly spelt word so....

STEP 3

Now take the second word from the second bracket:-

(out) + (like)   = 'outlike' ....this is not a properly spelt word so....

STEP 4

Now take the third word from the second bracket:-

(out) + (law)   = 'outlaw' ....yes, these two words joined together would make a properly spelt compound word!

So the answer must be 'out' and 'law'

 Mark the multiple choice answer box as shown:

If you had not been able to make a properly spelt word after having tried all of the words in the second bracket, you should then move on to the second word in the first bracket and then try again.

'Compound Words' – Example Questions

For these questions, join a word from the first group with a word from the second group to make a correctly spelt, new word. The word from the first group must always come first and the order of the letters must not be changed.

Example   Answer

    (out   up   down)   **out   law**   (the word is **outlaw**)
    (bite   like   law)

QUESTION 1

    (be   miss   men)
    (shone   have   tall)

1.
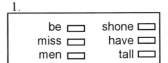

QUESTION 2

    (fox   pile   car)
    (rage   rot   ten)

2.
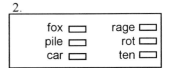

QUESTION 3

    (dam   full   knoll)
    (age   proof   sun)

3.
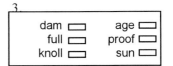

QUESTION 4

    (hair   an   bay)
    (enemy   gel   some)

4.
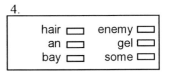

QUESTION 5

    (envy   ant   clean)
    (elope   nest   ironic)

5.

envy ▭	elope ▭
ant ▭	nest ▭
clean ▭	ironic ▭

QUESTION 6

(rim   hue   do)
(minnow   mastic   main)

6.

rim ▭	minnow ▭
hue ▭	mastic ▭
do ▭	main ▭

QUESTION 7

(garb   miss   know)
(ball   led   edge)

7.

garb ▭	ball ▭
miss ▭	led ▭
know ▭	edge ▭

QUESTION 8

(stum   gang   ham)
(stir   mock   ball)

8.

stum ▭	stir ▭
gang ▭	mock ▭
ham ▭	ball ▭

QUESTION 9

(mess   mast   miss)
(age   chief   sage)

9.

mess ▭	age ▭
mast ▭	chief ▭
miss ▭	sage ▭

QUESTION 10

(surf   off   beat)
(end   ten   fir)

10.

surf ▭	end ▭
off ▭	ten ▭
beat ▭	fir ▭

QUESTION 11

(sad   mud   pad)
(dell   pie   dock)

11.

sad ▭	dell ▭
mud ▭	pie ▭
pad ▭	dock ▭

QUESTION 12

(pall   mar   men)
(ace   rage   shone)

12.

pall ▭	ace ▭
mar ▭	rage ▭
men ▭	shone ▭

What do they look like?...

In the questions below there are two pairs of words.
On your answer sheet there are five words.
Mark one word on your answer sheet that will go
equally well with both pairs of words.

(modern   topical)
(flow   stream)

Multiple Choice Answer Box

movement ☐
contemporary ☐
current ☐
drift ☐
prevailing ☐

How to set about answering them...

In this question type you are looking for a word that has more than one meaning. This word is found in the multiple choice answer box and will fit with the two pairs of words that you have been given in the two brackets of the question.

The first thing to do is to read over the five possible answers in the multiple choice. If you don't immediately see a word there that can be associated with <u>both</u> of the pairs in the brackets, then you need to try each in turn.

Take the first word: Does it fit with the two words in the first bracket ? If so, then does it <u>also</u> fit with the two words in the second bracket ? If not, then try this method with the second word from the answer box. Continue through the list of the five words until you find a word that will fit with the two pairs of the words in brackets.

In the example here the word '**current**' will fit with the words in first bracket ('**modern**' & '**topical**') and it also has a second meaning which will fit well with the second bracket ('**flow**' & '**stream**').

The correct answers to this type of question will always be words that have more than one meaning.

Many English words have more than one meaning. Here are a few examples:-

axes   blow   close   desert   excuse   finish

Tips...

In your head, first eliminate the words in the multiple choice answer box that you feel sure are not the right answer. You can then focus on the remaining words.

'Words with More than One Meaning'
– Worked Example

The Question……

(instruct   teach)
(wagons   coaches)

The Answer Box……

learn ☐
bus ☐
educate ☐
passengers ☐
train ☐

STEP 1

Look for a word from the multiple choice answer box that goes well with all four words in the question:

Take each of the words from the multiple choice answer box in turn and compare them with the words in the question:

Try '**learn**'.   It is related to the words '**instruct**' and '**teach**' but it does not sit comfortably with the words '**wagons**' or '**coaches**' so move on to the next word:

Try '**bus**'.   This does not seem close in meaning to either of the words '**instruct**' or '**teach**' so move on to the next word:

Try '**educate**'.   The word '**educate**' is related to the words '**instruct**' and '**teach**' but is not related to the words '**wagons**' or '**coaches**' so move on to the next word:

Try '**passengers**'.   Whilst it is related to the words '**wagons**' or '**coaches**', it is not related in any obvious way to the words '**instruct**' or '**teach**' so move on again.

Try '**train**'.   Comparing it to the four words in the question, it is clear that '**train**' is related to both '**instruct**' & '**teach**' as well as '**wagons**' & '**coaches**'.

So '**train**' is the correct answer.

It is clear that the word '**train**' has more than one meaning. It is a noun, a thing that you can ride on, '*a train*' and it is also a verb, '*to train*' meaning to teach someone how to do something.

Mark the multiple choice answer box as shown: ⟹

learn ☐
bus ☐
educate ☐
passengers ☐
train ▤

'Words with More than One meaning'
– Example Questions

In the questions below there are two pairs of words.
On your answer sheet there are five words.
Mark one word on your answer sheet that will go equally well with both pairs of words.

Example   Answer

(modern   topical)   **current**
(flow   stream)

QUESTION 1

(climbed   ascended)
(flower   pink)

1.

petal ☐
mounted ☐
soared ☐
rose ☐
stem ☐

QUESTION 2

(rhythm   pulse)
(surpass   defeat)

2.

vibration ☐
victory ☐
challenge ☐
throb ☐
beat ☐

QUESTION 3

(nail   pin)
(saddle   bridle)

3.

tack ☐
horse ☐
heading ☐
hoof ☐
adhere ☐

QUESTION 4

(stopper   valve)
(strike   knock)

4.

percuss ☐
tap ☐
plug ☐
beat ☐
gate ☐

QUESTION 5

(shin   thigh)
(lamb   kid)

5.

puppy ☐
gosling ☐
ankle ☐
calf ☐
leg ☐

6.

silk	☐
touch	☐
linen	☐
felt	☐
aware	☐

QUESTION 6

(detected   perceived)
(cloth   baize)

7.

point	☐
aim	☐
objective	☐
decimal	☐
mark	☐

QUESTION 7

(purpose   reason)
(dot   spot)

8.

sunlight	☐
octopus	☐
ray	☐
bream	☐
torch	☐

QUESTION 8

(beam   shaft)
(catfish   shark)

9.

birth	☐
stern	☐
wake	☐
rear	☐
ridge	☐

QUESTION 9

(tail   back)
(raise   nurture)

10.

recuperate	☐
rest	☐
difference	☐
balance	☐
languish	☐

QUESTION 10

(relax   recover)
(remainder   remnants)

11.

enquire	☐
interrogate	☐
appeal	☐
gravitate	☐
examine	☐

QUESTION 11

(request   ask)
(draw   attract)

12.

contemporary	☐
impart	☐
present	☐
reigning	☐
contribute	☐

QUESTION 12

(current   existing)
(offer   provide)

'Complete the Sum'

What do they look like?...

In these questions you must find the number that will complete the sum correctly.
Find the correct number and mark it on the answer sheet.

$$5 + 8 = 9 + (?)$$

Multiple Choice Answer Box

2	▢
3	▢
4	▢
5	▢
6	▢

How to set about answering them...

In these questions you need to work along from the left of the sum to the right of the sum. Work out your sub-totals and mark them down onto the question sheet as you go.

The number that you arrive at for the right hand side of the sum needs to balance with the number you arrived at for the left hand side. Therefore it is a good idea to jot down the 'total' you arrived at for the left hand side and perhaps circle it so that it stands out amongst your other calculations.

Tips...

Being good at your times-tables really helps with these questions. Practice makes perfect !

Be especially careful when subtracting numbers. It's very easy to accidentally 'lose' or 'gain' 10.

Remember to work from left to right along the sum, working out the numbers as you go.

'Complete the Sum' – Worked Example

 The Question......

15 x 3 - 7 = 6 x 6 + (?)

The Answer Box......

STEP 1

 Begin by working out the left hand side of the sum as the unknown number (?) is on the right-hand side:

15 x 3 = 45 ⟶ 45 - 7 = 38

STEP 2

 Knowing that the left-hand side of the sum = 38, now look at the right-side:

38 = 6 x 6 + (?)   6 x 6 = 36 , so the sum now looks as follows:

38 = 36 + (?)   38 = 36 + **2**.

So the answer is '**2**'

 Mark the multiple choice answer box as shown ⟹

'Complete the Sum' – Example Questions

In these questions you must find the number that will complete the sum correctly. Find the correct number and mark it on the answer sheet.

Example   Answer

5   +   8   =   9   +   (?)   **4**

QUESTION 1

25   +   6   +   7   =   54   -   5   -   (?)

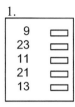

QUESTION 2

36   -   8   +   3   =   12   +   20   -   (?)

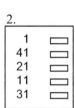

QUESTION 3

18   -   9   +   18   =   5   x   5   +   (?)

QUESTION 4

7   x   7   -   17   =   90   ÷   3   +   (?)

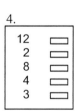

QUESTION 5

48   ÷   6   +   12   =   6   x   5   -   (?)

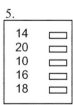

QUESTION 6

2   x   6   x   4   =   96   ÷   8   x   (?)

'Complete the Sum' – Example Questions

QUESTION 7

60 ÷ 15 x 8 = 8 x 8 - (?)

7.
22 ▭
32 ▭
12 ▭
28 ▭
18 ▭

QUESTION 8

7 x 9 + 14 = 35 + 25 + (?)

8.
27 ▭
17 ▭
7 ▭
14 ▭
13 ▭

QUESTION 9

31 + 48 + 12 = 8 x 9 + (?)

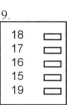

9.
18 ▭
17 ▭
16 ▭
15 ▭
19 ▭

QUESTION 10

42 - 13 - 7 = 50 - 18 - (?)

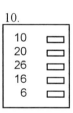

10.
10 ▭
20 ▭
26 ▭
16 ▭
6 ▭

QUESTION 11

160 ÷ 4 - 28 = 8 + 20 - (?)

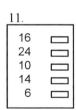

11.
16 ▭
24 ▭
10 ▭
14 ▭
6 ▭

QUESTION 12

15 x 2 - 11 = 76 ÷ 2 ÷ (?)

12.
3 ▭
4 ▭
5 ▭
10 ▭
2 ▭

'Letters for Numbers'

What do they look like?...

In these questions, letters stand for numbers. Work out the answer to each sum, then find the letter with that value and mark it on your answer sheet.

If A = 3, B = 6, C = 8, D = 1, E = 2,

what is the answer to this sum written as a letter ?

D + E + A = (?)

Multiple Choice Answer Box

A ☐
B ☐
C ☐
D ☐
E ☐

How to set about answering them...

In these questions, letters stand for numbers. You need to work out the answer to the sum and give your answer as a letter.

It always helps if you write the numbers over the letters. This makes it easier for you to work out the sum as you do not have to keep checking the value of each letter.

When you have worked out the answer to the sum, find the letter which represents your number in the question and mark this letter on the multiple choice answer sheet.

Do not try to do all of the calculations in your head. You are more likely to make mistakes if you do this. Remember that you can use the question sheet for any rough workings.

Tips...

Write the numbers over the letters in each sum.

If, say, the letters 'A', 'B', 'C' and 'D' are used in the sum, don't simply assume that the answer has to be the letter 'E'. The correct answer could be one of the letters already used in the sum.

'Letters for Numbers' - Worked Example

The Question......

The Answer Box......

If A = 24, B= 36, C = 8, D = 48, E = 6,
what is the answer to this sum written as a letter ?

E x C - A = (?)

STEP 1

Begin by writing the numbers above the letters.

$$6 \quad 8 \quad 24$$
$$E \times C - A = (?)$$

From these numbers you are now able to calculate the sum.

$$6 \times 8 - 24 = (?)$$

$$6 \times 8 = 48$$

$$48 - 24 = \textbf{24}$$

STEP 2

Once you have calculated the sum you will need to refer back to the question and look to see which letter equals your answer.

In this case **A** = 24.

So the answer is '**A**'.

 Mark the multiple choice answer box as shown

'Letters for Numbers' – Example Questions

In these questions, letters stand for numbers.
Work out the answer to each sum, then find the letter with that value and mark it on your answer sheet.

Example

    If A = 3, B = 6, C = 8, D = 1, E = 2,
    what is the answer to this sum written as a letter ?
    D + E + A = (?)

Answer

B

QUESTION 1

If A = 3, B = 4, C = 5, D = 6, E = 8,
what is the answer to this sum written as a letter ?
A + C - B = (?)

QUESTION 2

If A = 3, B = 5, C = 8, D = 10, E = 16,
what is the answer to this sum written as a letter ?
E ÷ C + A = (?)

QUESTION 3

If A = 2, B = 200, C = 10, D = 20, E = 12,
what is the answer to this sum written as a letter ?
D ÷ C x C = (?)

QUESTION 4

If A = 12, B = 8, C = 26, D = 5, E = 16,
what is the answer to this sum written as a letter ?
B x D - A - A = (?)

QUESTION 5

If A = 7, B = 24, C = 20, D = 2, E = 6,
what is the answer to this sum written as a letter ?
A x E + D - B = (?)

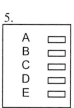

QUESTION 6

If A = 15, B = 13, C = 12, D = 18, E = 8,
what is the answer to this sum written as a letter ?
D - B + A - E = (?)

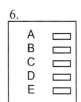

QUESTION 7

If A = 30, B = 12, C = 5, D = 10, E = 3,
what is the answer to this sum written as a letter ?
A ÷ E ÷ C + D = (?)

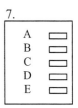

QUESTION 8

If A = 18, B = 12, C = 3, D = 8, E = 32,
what is the answer to this sum written as a letter ?
E ÷ D x C + D - B = (?)

QUESTION 9

If A = 20, B = 5, C = 30, D = 120, E = 24,
what is the answer to this sum written as a letter ?
D ÷ E x B - B = (?)

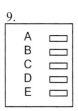

QUESTION 10

If A = 6, B = 3, C = 2, D = 4, E = 12,
what is the answer to this sum written as a letter ?
A ÷ B x C = (?)

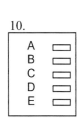

QUESTION 11

If A = 32, B = 18, C = 7, D = 9, E = 30,
what is the answer to this sum written as a letter ?
A - B + C + D = (?)

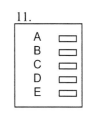

QUESTION 12

If A = 4, B = 5, C = 6, D = 20, E = 36,
what is the answer to this sum written as a letter ?
E ÷ C + A - B = (?)

What do they look like?...

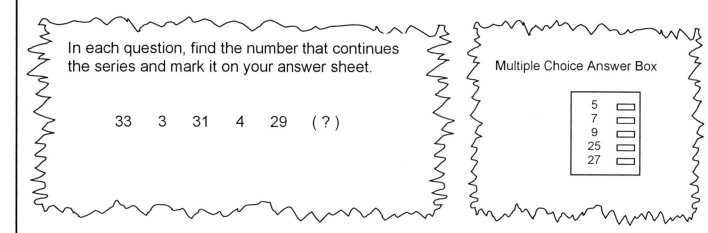

In each question, find the number that continues the series and mark it on your answer sheet.

33   3   31   4   29   (?)

Multiple Choice Answer Box

5 ☐
7 ☐
9 ☐
25 ☐
27 ☐

How to set about answering them...

For these questions you need to discover the patterns and to put in a number at the end of the series to continue the pattern.

First look at the whole row of numbers. Do they appear to be increasing or decreasing ? You may immediately see the pattern.

Next look to see if the numbers 'leapfrog'. Does the pattern jump from one number, skip one and go on to the next ?

When you have decided how the pattern runs, look at the size of the increase or decrease in the numbers. Can you see the pattern ?

Do they run on by adding, subtracting, multiplying or even dividing ?

Tips...

When you have found the pattern, write the numbers and signs (+ , - , x , ÷) between the numbers in the question. This helps to prevent careless mistakes.

If you have discovered that the numbers 'leapfrog', draw arrows between the alternate 'leapfrogging' numbers to help prevent giving a careless answer at the end of the row.

'Number Patterns' - Worked Example

The Question......

The Answer Box......

14	▭
16	▭
17	▭
18	▭
20	▭

15   18   16   19   17   (?)

STEP 1

Look at the number pattern to see if there is an obvious relationship between the adjacent numbers in the series.

There is not. The numbers are all quite close in value so it seems unlikely that the series involves multiplication or division.

STEP 2

Look at how the adjacent numbers relate in terms of addition and subtraction.

Starting on the left and moving along the series, write the change in value of each pair of adjacent numbers above.

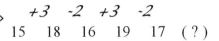

```
   +3   -2   +3   -2
15   18   16   19   17   ( ? )
```

Having done this, you can see that the pattern is +3, -2, +3 -2 and so on.

The next change in value, therefore, will be '+3'.

STEP 3

Add 3 to 17 to find the next number in the series and therefore, the answer.

> So the answer is **20.**

 Mark the multiple choice answer box as shown

14	▭
16	▭
17	▭
18	▭
20	▱

In each question, find the number that continues the series and mark it on your answer sheet.

Example   Answer

    4   8   12   16   20 (?)   **24**

QUESTION 1

    3   4   6   9   13 (?)

1.

17	☐
18	☐
19	☐
21	☐
22	☐

QUESTION 2

    2   4   8   14   22 (?)

2.

24	☐
26	☐
28	☐
30	☐
32	☐

QUESTION 3

    10   15   18   23   26 (?)

3.

29	☐
31	☐
33	☐
34	☐
35	☐

QUESTION 4

    27   24   20   17   13 (?)

4.

7	☐
8	☐
9	☐
10	☐
11	☐

QUESTION 5

    13   15   10   12   7 (?)

5.

6	☐
7	☐
8	☐
9	☐
10	☐

'Number Patterns' – Example Questions

QUESTION 6

64   32   16   8   4   (?)

6.

0	☐
1	☐
2	☐
3	☐
4	☐

QUESTION 7

30   28   25   23   20   (?)

7.

22	☐
21	☐
20	☐
19	☐
18	☐

QUESTION 8

5   10   12   24   19   (?)

8.

18	☐
28	☐
38	☐
48	☐
58	☐

QUESTION 9

18   13   17   14   16   (?)

9.

15	☐
16	☐
17	☐
18	☐
19	☐

QUESTION 10

12   14   24   26   36   (?)

10.

28	☐
34	☐
38	☐
40	☐
42	☐

QUESTION 11

2   4   12   24   72   (?)

11.

84	☐
108	☐
124	☐
132	☐
144	☐

QUESTION 12

10   19   27   34   40   (?)

12.

44	☐
45	☐
48	☐
49	☐
50	☐

'Missing Number'

What do they look like?...

In these questions, the three numbers in each group below are related in the same way.
The first two groups have been completed for you. Find the rule that connects the numbers in the first two groups and then use this rule to find the missing number in the third group. Mark this number on your answer sheet.

(5 [10] 2)   (6 [24] 4)
(8 [?] 2)

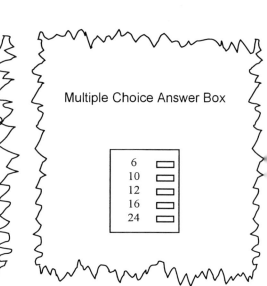

Multiple Choice Answer Box

6
10
12
16
24

How to set about answering them...

In these questions, the number in the centre of the first two groups has been made by using the two <u>outer</u> numbers of these groups. You need to find the missing number in the third group by using the same method as used in the first two groups.

Look at it this way....   (A (C) B)   A and B are used to make C.

In the example above, in the first group (5 [10] 2) it can be seen that 5 x 2 =10. A and B are multiplied together to make C (A x B =C).

You must then <u>check</u> the second group to see if the <u>same</u> method can be used:-

In the second group (6 [24] 4) it can be seen that 6 x 4 =24. Again, A and B are multiplied together to make C (A x B =C).

If it seems that the same method works for the first and second groups, then you need to apply this method to the third group (8 [?] 2). 8 x 2 = 16.

So the missing number in the third group is 16.

Tips...

There can often be more than one way to relate the three numbers within a bracket. So as soon as you think you've worked out how the numbers in the first bracket are related, check that the same relationship works with the second bracket. If the relationship doesn't work on the second bracket, go back to the first bracket and look for another way to link the three numbers.
Remember that the relationship can include both addition or subtraction as well as multiplication or division. For example, you may have to multiply the two numbers on the outside of the bracket and then add, subtract, multiply or divide by another number to arrive to the number in the middle.

'Missing Number' - Worked Example

 The Question...... The Answer Box......

(3 [8] 4)   (4 [15] 5)
(5 [?] 6)

12	▭
24	▭
11	▭
48	▭
28	▭

STEP 1

Look at the three numbers in the first group. It is not simply the addition of A and B as 3 + 4 =7 (not 8). Equally, it is not subtraction of A from B as 4 – 3 = 1 (not 8). Nor is it multiplication of A and B as 3 x 4 =12 (not 8). And it isn't division as neither 3 ÷ 4 nor 4 ÷ 3 =8. So you need to think of a more complicated relationship between the numbers.
Looking at the numbers 3, 4 and 8, it could be that the relationship between A, B and C is:-

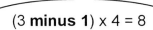

(**3 minus 1**) x 4 = 8   Or written another way ...   (A **– 1**) x B = C

OR ...

3 + 4 **plus 1** = 8   Or written another way ...   A + B **+ 1** = C

...or one of many other combinations, but the important thing is that you find the one that also works with the second group

STEP 2

So you need to try each of the above with the second group to see if any of them work equally well.

If you take the first of the possible relationships written down above, **(A – 1) x B = C** , and try to apply it to the second group you will find that.....

(4 - 1) x 5 =15   Yes, this relationship also works for the second group.

STEP 3

You can now apply this relationship to the third group **(5 [?] 6)** to find the missing number.

(5 - 1) x 6 = 24   So the missing number is **24** and the group would be written **(5 (24) 6)**

So the answer is '**24**'.

 Mark the multiple choice answer box as shown ⇒

12	▭
24	▬
11	▭
48	▭
28	▭

In these questions, the three numbers in each group below are related in the same way. The first two groups have been completed for you.
Find the rule that connects the numbers in the first two groups and then use this rule to find the missing number in the third group. Mark this number on your answer sheet.

Example
(5 [10] 2)   (6 [24] 4)
(8 [?] 2)

Answer
16

QUESTION 1

(5 [8] 3)   (4 [9] 5)
(8 [?] 3)

1.
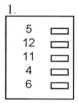

5
12
11
4
6

QUESTION 2

(12 [6] 6)   (15 [10] 5)
(16 [?] 7)

2.
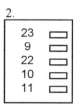

23
9
22
10
11

QUESTION 3

(2 [2] 4)   (4 [12] 16)
(8 [?] 12)

3.
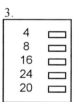

4
8
16
24
20

QUESTION 4

(2 [6] 3)   (3 [12] 4)
(7 [?] 6)

4.
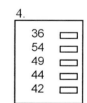

36
54
49
44
42

QUESTION 5

(4 [2] 2)   (16 [4] 4)
(24 [?] 8)

5.
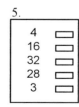

4
16
32
28
3

'Missing Number' - Example Questions

QUESTION 6

(8 [5] 40)   (9 [6] 54)
(7 [?] 63)

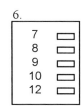

6.

7	
8	
9	
10	
12	

QUESTION 7

(3 [24] 4)   (5 [40] 4)
(2 [?] 9)

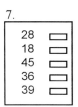

7.

28	
18	
45	
36	
39	

QUESTION 8

(3 [11] 6)   (4 [18] 12)
(16 [?] 7)

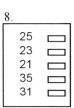

8.

25	
23	
21	
35	
31	

QUESTION 9

(30 [15] 5)   (60 [10] 40)
(35 [?] 15)

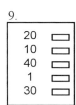

9.

20	
10	
40	
1	
30	

QUESTION 10

(20 [20] 10)   (28 [20] 6)
(36 [?] 12)

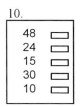

10.

48	
24	
15	
30	
10	

QUESTION 11

(4 [16] 8)   (7 [21] 6)
(5 [?] 8)

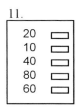

11.

20	
10	
40	
80	
60	

QUESTION 12

(20 [40] 40)   (13 [20] 14)
(15 [?] 16)

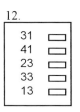

12.

31	
41	
23	
33	
13	

What do they look like?...

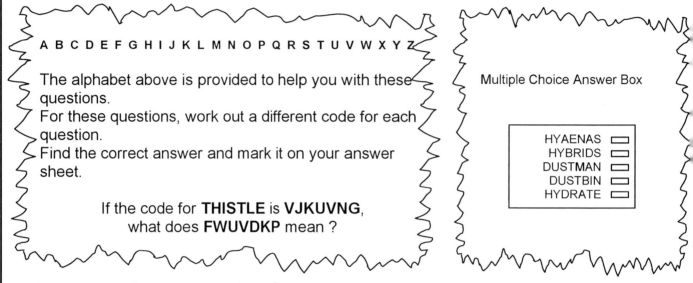

A B C D E F G H I J K L M N O P Q R S T U V W X Y Z

The alphabet above is provided to help you with these questions.
For these questions, work out a different code for each question.
Find the correct answer and mark it on your answer sheet.

If the code for **THISTLE** is **VJKUVNG**,
what does **FWUVDKP** mean ?

Multiple Choice Answer Box

HYAENAS	☐
HYBRIDS	☐
DUSTMAN	☐
DUSTBIN	☐
HYDRATE	☐

How to set about answering them...

For these questions, you need to crack the code and then use that same code to find the missing word or code. When you set the question out clearly as below, you can see that the 'T' of 'THISTLE' is represented by a 'V'. By counting back two places in the alphabet from 'V' you will arrive at 'T'. Following the same code, the 'F' would be represented as a 'D' at the start of your answer. Now continue to crack the code for each of the other letters.

V J K U V N G	F W U V D K
T H I S T L E	D

Tips...

Every question will use a different code so remember that you will have to work it out each time you move to a new question.

Use the alphabet provided at the top of the questions to help you count up and down.

Help yourself to count correctly along the alphabet by tapping quietly along with your pencil, rather than just using your eyes.

Remember to look out for 'mirror image' codes – for example where 'Z' is the code for 'A', 'Y' is the code for 'B' etc.

In some questions, the code is different for each letter so don't assume that the code on the first letter necessarily continues along the whole word.

A B C D E F G H I J K L M N O P Q R S T U V W X Y Z

The Question……

The Answer Box……

If the code for **CLAW** is **DMBX**,
what is the code for **LAMB** ?

MALC	☐
KBNC	☐
MBNC	☐
MBLC	☐
KCNC	☐

STEP 1

Firstly, draw a grid and enter the words and codes that you have been given (words at the top and codes at the bottom).

C L A W	L A M B
D M B X	

You can see that the code for '**CLAW**' has been created by adding one letter in the alphabet:
The letter '**C**' has become '**D**', the letter '**L**' has become '**M**' and so on.

STEP 2

To work out the code for the word '**LAMB**', you must do the same for each of its letters as had been done for the word '**CLAW**'

The letter '**L**' becomes '**M**', the letter '**A**' becomes '**B**' etc.

Write the codes onto your grid:

C L A W	L A M B
D M B X	M B N C

So the answer is '**MBNC**'.

Mark the multiple choice answer box as shown.

MALC	☐
KBNC	☐
MBNC	▭
MBLC	☐
KCNC	☐

A B C D E F G H I J K L M N O P Q R S T U V W X Y Z

The alphabet above is provided to help you with these questions.
For these questions, work out a different code for each question.
Find the correct answer and mark it on your answer sheet.

Example	Answer
If the code for **THISTLE** is **VJKUVNG**, what does **FWUVDKP** mean ?	**DUSTBIN**

QUESTION 1

If the code for **CATS** is **DBUT**, what is the code for **DOGS** ?

1.
- EPTH ▢
- EPHT ▢
- ENTH ▢
- CPHT ▢
- CNTH ▢

QUESTION 2

If the code for **HASP** is **GZRO**, what does **KNBJ** mean ?

2.
- JACK ▢
- LUCK ▢
- LOCK ▢
- JAYS ▢
- LOSE ▢

QUESTION 3

If the code for **PITCH** is **QHUBI**, what is the code for **BLACK** ?

3.
- CKBBL ▢
- CMBLB ▢
- AKCLB ▢
- AMBBL ▢
- AKCBL ▢

QUESTION 4

If the code for **PLANT** is **RKCMV**, what does **UGTTD** mean ?

4.
- SHOUT ▢
- SHEET ▢
- SHOES ▢
- SHRUB ▢
- SHIRE ▢

QUESTION 5

If **VFDUO** is the code for **SHAWL**, what is the code for **SKIRT** ?

5.
- VILPW ▢
- PILWP ▢
- PMLPW ▢
- VMLWP ▢
- PIPLW ▢

QUESTION 6

If **SQBEQ** is the code for **ROYAL**,
what does **GNXWM** mean ?

6.

PRINCE	▭
FLASH	▭
HORSE	▭
HOUSE	▭
FLUSH	▭

QUESTION 7

If **RFLQO** is the code for **SHOUT**,
what is **ROUND** in code ?

7.

QWERT	▭
QMRJY	▭
QRTJY	▭
SRTJY	▭
RMRTY	▭

QUESTION 8

If the code for **SWEET** is **OZZHN**,
what does **PRJWB** mean ?

8.

SUGAR	▭
TOOLS	▭
TOOTH	▭
TEETH	▭
TALES	▭

QUESTION 9

If **SUGAR** in code is **TSJWW**,
what is the code for **SPICE** ?

9.

TRLMP	▭
SPKPE	▭
TNLYJ	▭
TNYJL	▭
RNJYL	▭

QUESTION 10

If **RCXRE** is the code for **PETTY**,
what does **RMMQK** mean ?

10.

POKER	▭
QUEEN	▭
PRIZE	▭
QUICK	▭
POISE	▭

QUESTION 11

If **OLMPB** is the code for **MOIST**,
what is the code for **RISER** ?

11.

RKYBZ	▭
TFWBZ	▭
RFWZB	▭
PFWGS	▭
TYKGS	▭

QUESTION 12

If **HABIT** in code is **CEYKS**,
what does **VFYGX** mean ?

12.

ABBEY	▭
ABODE	▭
ABOUT	▭
AXIOM	▭
AXLES	▭

What do they look like?...

In these questions, there are four words and the codes for **three** of them are shown.
These codes are **not** written in the same order as the words and one of the codes is missing.

LEE   ALE   EAT   ATE
413   423   342

Work out the correct code for each word and then answer the following questions.

Which word has the number code **413** ?

Multiple Choice Answer Box

TEA ☐
EAT ☐
ALE ☐
ATE ☐
LEE ☐

How to set about answering them...

Here you need to crack the code by matching up the three groups of numbers with their corresponding word.

Look at the frequency of the numbers. Do any of the numbers appear quite frequently and seem to appear in the same position as any of the letters in the words?

Here the number '**4**' begins two groups and the letter '**A**' begins two words, therefore it is likely that the words '**ALE**' and '**ATE**' are represented by the codes '**413**' and '**423**'. However, at this stage we cannot be sure which code represents which word.

Now look at '**ALE**' and '**ATE**' more closely: After establishing that the letter '**A**' is the number '**4**', it seems that '**342**' should be matched with '**EAT**' as there is an '**A**' in the middle of '**EAT**' and a '**4**' in the middle of '**342**'.

Using this information you can now establish that the letter '**T**' is represented by the number '**2**', matching '**ATE**' to '**423**', and therefore indicating '**ALE**' as the match to '**413**'.

Using this method work through each of the letters and numbers to match them up.

Tips...

Look first for any double letters – a very good hint if there are two numbers together.

Once you have matched a number with a letter, write the number above the letter wherever it appears in the words. This will help you to quickly build a clearer picture of the words and their codes.

'Word Codes 2' - Worked Example

The Question......   The Answer Box......

POLE   PEAR   LEAP   REAL
    5231   6143   5146
Which word has the number code **6143** ?

POLE	▭
PEAR	▭
LEAP	▭
REAL	▭
PARE	▭

STEP 1

Look at the three number codes that you have been given.

You will notice that two of them begin with the same number, '**5**'. This is helpful as two of the words above them begin with the same letter, '**P**'. So straight away you know that the code for '**P**' is '**5**'.

Write the number '**5**' above every letter '**P**'.

STEP 2

Now look to see if you can work out which word beginning with the letter '**P**' and which code beginning with the number '**5**' can be matched together.

Looking to the second number in each of the codes beginning with '**5**', you will notice that one of the codes has a number '**2**' as its second number and one has a number '**1**' as its second number. But the third code (**6143**) also has a number '**1**' as its second number. This means that the word that has the code '**5146**', has the same second letter as the word with the code '**6143**'.

Looking at the four words above, three of them have the same second letter, '**E**' and only one has an '**O**' as its second letter.

This means that the number code '**5146**' must relate to a word beginning with the letters '**PE**'. There is only one word beginning with the letters '**PE**' and that is '**PEAR**'.

Now write the number '**1**' above every letter '**E**'. Also, write the number '**4**' above every letter '**A**' and the number '**6**' above every letter '**R**'.

You also know that the other code beginning with the number '**5**' (**5231**) must relate to the other word beginning with '**P**' and that is '**POLE**'.

Now write the number '**2**' above every letter '**O**'. Also write the number '**3**' above every letter '**L**'.

Your question sheet should now look like this:

5231   5146   3145   6143
POLE   PEAR   LEAP   REAL
    5231   6143   5146

So, returning to the question: 'Which word has the number code **6143** ?' ......**REAL**

Mark the multiple choice answer box as shown.

POLE	▭
PEAR	▭
LEAP	▭
REAL	▤
PARE	▭

Copyright © PHI Education 2012

In these questions, there are four words and the codes for **three** of them are shown.
These codes are **not** written in the same order as the words and one of the codes is missing.

> POLE   PEAR   LEAP   REAL
> 5231   6143   5146

Work out the correct code for each word and then answer the following questions.
Mark the correct answers on your answer sheet.

Example   Answer

Which word has the number code **5231** ?   **POLE**

QUESTION 1

Which word has the number code **6143** ?

1

POLE	☐
PEAR	☐
LEAP	☐
REAL	☐
PARE	☐

QUESTION 2

What is the number code for the word **PEAR** ?

2

3145	☐
5231	☐
5146	☐
6143	☐
5461	☐

QUESTION 3

What is the number code for the word **PARE** ?

3

3145	☐
5231	☐
5146	☐
6143	☐
5461	☐

Again, work out the correct code for each word below and then answer the following questions.
Mark the correct answers on your answer sheet.

> SOUP   POST   STUD   DUPE
> 5423   6745   6142

QUESTION 4

What is the number code for the word **POST** ?

4

7136	☐
6142	☐
5423	☐
2167	☐
6745	☐

QUESTION 5

Which word has the code **6142** ?

5

SOUP	☐
POST	☐
STUD	☐
DUPE	☐
TOES	☐

'Word Codes 2' – Example Questions

QUESTION 6

What is the word for the code **7136** ?

6
SOUP	☐
POST	☐
STUD	☐
DUPE	☐
TOES	☐

Again, work out the correct code for each word below and then answer the following questions. Mark the correct answers on your answer sheet.

        MOAT   LACE   MOLE   COAL
          1537   3267   1524

QUESTION 7

Which word has the number code **1524** ?

7
MOAT	☐
LACE	☐
MOLE	☐
COAL	☐
LAME	☐

QUESTION 8

What is the number code for the word **COAL** ?

8
3217	☐
1537	☐
3267	☐
1524	☐
6523	☐

QUESTION 9

What is the number code for the word **LAME** ?

9
3217	☐
1537	☐
3267	☐
1524	☐
6523	☐

Again, work out the correct code for each word below and then answer the following questions. Mark the correct answers on your answer sheet.

        SPIN   PINE   PIES   SINE
          4513   4521   3521

QUESTION 10

What is the number code for the word **NINE** ?

10
3521	☐
4513	☐
2521	☐
3452	☐
4521	☐

QUESTION 11

Which word has the code **3452** ?

11
SPIN	☐
PINE	☐
PIES	☐
SINE	☐
NINE	☐

QUESTION 12

What is the word for the code **4513** ?

12
SPIN	☐
PINE	☐
PIES	☐
SINE	☐
NINE	☐

'Alphabet Codes'

What do they look like?...

A B C D E F G H I J K L M N O P Q R S T U V W X Y Z
The alphabet above is provided to help you with these questions.
For these questions, find the letters that complete the statement in the best way and mark the answer on your answer sheet.

CD is to **EF**
as **PQ** is to (?).

Multiple Choice Answer Box

PR ☐
QP ☐
QR ☐
RS ☐
PS ☐

How to set about answering them...

With these questions you need to complete the sentence by finding the <u>two</u> missing letters.

You need to take the <u>first</u> letter of both pairs on the top line and look at what has happened in the alphabet. In the example above to move from '**C**' to '**E**' you have to jump two places forward in the alphabet.

Taking this information and still dealing with the first letters, you need to move down to the line below and apply the same change. If you take the letter '**P**' and then move two places forward in the alphabet, you arrive at '**R**'. This is the first letter of your answer.

Now, you take the <u>second</u> letter of the top line. In the example above look to see what has happened to the second letter. To move from '**D**' to '**F**' it has moved forward two places in the alphabet.

As before, move down to the second line and take the second letter '**Q**' and then move forward two places to the letter '**S**'. This is the second letter of your answer. Your answer is '**RS**'.

Tips...

Write the size of the gap between the first letters of each pair above them and the gap between the second letters of each pair below. Whilst, in the example above, both the first and second letters jumped forwards two places, the size and direction of the gaps between the first and second letter of each pair, may well differ.

Use the alphabet provided on the question sheet to work out the gaps between the letters.

Tap your pencil quietly along the alphabet to help you count accurately. Just using your eyes to count along can result in careless mistakes.

'Alphabet Codes' – Worked Example

A B C D E F G H I J K L M N O P Q R S T U V W X Y Z

The Question……

PH is to **LK**
as **EM** is to (?).

The Answer Box……

BR ☐
AR ☐
BP ☐
AP ☐
BS ☐

STEP 1

You need to look at the top line and consider the first letters of each pair - '**P**' and '**L**'.

To move from '**P**' to '**L**' you need to move backwards through the alphabet four places. Write ' **- 4**' above the letter '**P**' on the question sheet.

Now move down to the bottom line and, taking the first letter '**E**', move backwards through the alphabet four places to '**A**'. This is the first letter of your answer. Write it down by the (?) on the bottom line.

STEP 2

Now, moving back to the top line, look at the second letters of each pair - '**H**' and '**K**'.

To move from '**H**' to '**K**' you need to move forwards through the alphabet three places. Write '**+3**' above the letter '**H**'.

Now move down again to the bottom line and, taking the second letter '**M**', move forwards through the alphabet three places to '**P**'. This is the second letter of your answer. Write it next to (to the right) the letter '**A**' to make '**AP**'.

-4 +3   -4 +3
PH is to LK as EM is to '**AP**'.

So the answer is '**AP**'

Mark the multiple choice answer box as shown: ⟹

BR ☐
AR ☐
BP ☐
AP ☰
BS ☐

'Alphabet Codes' – Example Questions

A B C D E F G H I J K L M N O P Q R S T U V W X Y Z

The alphabet above is provided to help you with these questions.
For these questions, find the letters that complete the statement in the best way and mark the answer on your answer sheet.

Example	Answer
CD is to **EF** as **PQ** is to (?).	**RS**

QUESTION 1

CF is to **DG**
as **EH** is to (?).

1.
EF ▭
FI ▭
DH ▭
DI ▭
FJ ▭

QUESTION 2

GK is to **HJ**
as **FI** is to (?).

2.
FJ ▭
GJ ▭
GH ▭
FH ▭
GK ▭

QUESTION 3

BA is to **GB**
as **DM** is to (?).

3.
HR ▭
ER ▭
EN ▭
HL ▭
IN ▭

QUESTION 4

QC is to **TA**
as **TD** is to (?).

4.
WA ▭
WB ▭
WC ▭
WF ▭
WG ▭

QUESTION 5

NW is to **JS**
as **OF** is to (?).

5.
KB ▭
KJ ▭
BK ▭
SJ ▭
SB ▭

QUESTION 6

LS is to **IX**
as **IX** is to (?).

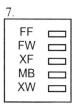

6.
AC	☐
AS	☐
FC	☐
FS	☐
LS	☐

QUESTION 7

BD is to **YX**
as **AC** is to (?).

7.
FF	☐
FW	☐
XF	☐
MB	☐
XW	☐

QUESTION 8

CF is to **XK**
as **QL** is to (?).

8.
QL	☐
VL	☐
VQ	☐
LQ	☐
VG	☐

QUESTION 9

VE is to **ZA**
as **ZA** is to (?).

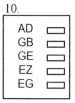

9.
VW	☐
VE	☐
DE	☐
DW	☐
AZ	☐

QUESTION 10

HZ is to **EA**
as **DC** is to (?).

10.
AD	☐
GB	☐
GE	☐
EZ	☐
EG	☐

QUESTION 11

XB is to **CX**
as **PP** is to (?).

11.
UT	☐
UK	☐
TK	☐
TL	☐
UL	☐

QUESTION 12

PM is to **MK**
as **PK** is to (?).

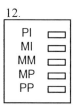

12.
PI	☐
MI	☐
MM	☐
MP	☐
PP	☐

What do they look like?...

A B C D E F G H I J K L M N O P Q R S T U V W X Y Z

The alphabet above is provided to help you with these questions.
For these questions, find the next pair of letters for each series and mark the correct answer on your answer sheet.

BZ   CY   DX   EW   FV   (?)

Multiple Choice Answer Box

FT ☐
EU ☐
GU ☐
GT ☐
FW ☐

How to set about answering them...

With these questions you need to continue the letter series to find the next two letters by using your alphabet.

For example: **BZ   CY   DX   EW   FV   (?)**

Glance along the whole line first, you may be lucky and see the pattern immediately.

If not, then the best way to start is to divide the pairs into the first and second letters.

Deal with the first letters first: **B   C   D   E   F   (?)**

You can see that the pattern has moved <u>forward one</u> letter each time.

If you continue the pattern you can see that the first letter of the next pair would be **'G'**.

Now deal with the second letters: **Z   Y   X   W   V   (?)**

You can see that the pattern has moved <u>back one</u> letter each time.

If you continue the pattern you can see that the second letter of the next pair would be **'U'**.

Therefore, the missing letter pair is **'GU'**

Tips...

Write the size of the gap between the first letters of each pair above them and the gap between the second letters of each pair below. The size of the gaps may change along the pattern.

Tap your pencil quietly along the alphabet to help you count accurately. Just using your eyes to count along can result in careless mistakes.

'Letter Patterns' - Worked Example

A B C D E F G H I J K L M N O P Q R S T U V W X Y Z

The Question......

AM CO EQ GS IU (?)

The Answer Box......

KX ▭
JV ▭
JX ▭
KW ▭
LV ▭

STEP 1

You need to look at the first letters making up each letter pair, 'A', 'C', 'E', 'G' and 'I'.

To move from 'A' to 'C' to 'E' to 'G' to 'I' you need to move forwards through the alphabet two places each time.

Write **' +2**' above the first letters in each letter pair on the question sheet.

+2 *+2* *+2* *+2* *+2*

AM CO EQ GS IU (*K* *?*)

STEP 2

Now, you need to look at the second letters of each letter pair, 'M', 'O', 'Q', 'S' and 'U'.

Again, these have moved two places forwards through the alphabet each time.

Write '+2' below the second letters in each letter pair on the question sheet.

+2 *+2* *+2* *+2* *+2*

AM CO EQ GS IU (*K* *W*)

+2 *+2* *+2* *+2* *+2*

:

So the answer is **KW**

Mark the multiple choice answer box as shown:

KX ▭
JV ▭
JX ▭
KW ▤
LV ▭

'Letter Patterns' – Example Questions

A B C D E F G H I J K L M N O P Q R S T U V W X Y Z

The alphabet above is provided to help you with these questions.
For these questions, find the letters that continue the pattern in the best way and mark the answer on your answer sheet.

Example   Answer

    BZ CY DX EW FV (?)   **GU**

QUESTION 1

    DN EO FP GQ HR (?)

QUESTION 2

    SR QP ON ML KJ (?)

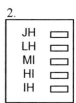

QUESTION 3

    FV DX BZ ZB XD (?)

QUESTION 4

    KT MS OR QQ SP (?)

QUESTION 5

    BY EV HS KP NM (?)

QUESTION 6

JA KB MC PD TE (?)

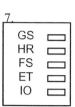

6.
WF	☐
ZF	☐
YF	☐
WE	☐
ZE	☐

QUESTION 7

UH TG RE OB KX (?)

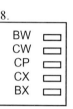

7.
GS	☐
HR	☐
FS	☐
ET	☐
IO	☐

QUESTION 8

HC GE FH EL DQ (?)

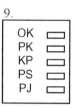

8.
BW	☐
CW	☐
CP	☐
CX	☐
BX	☐

QUESTION 9

AZ BY DW GT KP (?)

9.
OK	☐
PK	☐
KP	☐
PS	☐
PJ	☐

QUESTION 10

OO SJ WF AC EA (?)

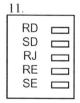

10.
JZ	☐
IA	☐
IX	☐
IB	☐
IZ	☐

QUESTION 11

CX HV LS OO QJ (?)

11.
RD	☐
SD	☐
RJ	☐
RE	☐
SE	☐

QUESTION 12

CC ZG WK TO QS (?)

12.
NT	☐
WN	☐
NU	☐
NW	☐
XN	☐

'Words from Other Words 1'

What do they look like?...

In these questions, there are three pairs of words in brackets.
The second word, in each of the first two brackets, has been formed using some of the letters from the first word.
Find the missing word in the third bracket by using the same method as used in the first two brackets. Mark the correct answer on your answer sheet.

(catches   each)   (naively   lane)
(magnetic   [?])

Multiple Choice Answer Box

tame   ▭
neat   ▭
team   ▭
time   ▭
name   ▭

How to set about answering them...

In each of the three brackets, a second word is been formed by selecting letters from the first word. The same pattern has been used for the first two brackets and you need to follow that same pattern to find the missing word in the third bracket.

In the example it can probably be seen at a glance that the sixth, second, first and fifth letters of the first words in the first two brackets have been used to make the second words. Therefore it is reasonably easy to pick out the sixth, second, first and fifth letters of the third bracket to make the word '**tame**'.

Of course these questions can be much trickier and then the method of writing the relevant position numbers over the letters of the second word in each bracket, is the best to be used.

As the letters of '**each**' are the sixth, second, first and fifth letters of the word '**catches**', write the numbers '**6**', '**2**', '**1**' and '**5**' over the letters '**e**', '**a**', '**c**' and '**h**' of the word '**each**', respectively.

Do the same for '**l**', '**a**', '**n**' and '**e**' in the second bracket as these are the sixth, second, first and fifth letters of the word '**naively**'.

Now write '**6**', '**2**', '**1**' and '**5**' in the missing bracket and then write the respective sixth, second, first and fifth letters of '**magnetic**' underneath those numbers.

This is a good method to adopt for these questions as they can become too complex to work out in your head.

Tips...

A letter used in the second word of a bracket, may be seen more than once in the first word within that bracket. When this occurs, write down the positions of both of the letters above the letter in the second word. Do this for both the first and second set of brackets and then see which relationship is common to both sets of brackets.

'Words from Other Words 1' - Worked Example

The Question……

(piglet   pet)   (driven   den)
(astute   [?])

The Answer Box……

tea ☐
eat ☐
sat ☐
ate ☐
set ☐

STEP 1

Look at the words in the first bracket.

Thinking about the derived word '**pet**', you can see straight away that there is only one '**p**', one '**e**' and one '**t**' in the first word this is helpful as there can only be one way to derive the letters in the second word.

Taking each letter from the word '**pet**' in turn:

The letter '**p**' is the **first** letter in the first word, the letter '**e**' is the **fifth** letter in the first word and the letter '**t**' is the **sixth** letter in the first word.

Write the numbers '**1**', '**5**' & '**6**' over the letters '**p**', '**e**' & '**t**'

STEP 2

Look now at the second bracket, you should see the same relationship:

Taking each letter from the word '**den**' in turn:

The letter '**d**' is the **first** letter in the first word, the letter '**e**' is the **fifth** letter in the first word and the letter '**n**' is the **sixth** letter in the first word.

The relationship is the same – '**1**', '**5**' & '**6**'.

STEP 3

Now apply this rule to the third bracket:

Write the numbers '**1**', '**5**' & '**6**' and then copy the **first**, **fifth** and **sixth** letters of the word '**astute**' under them.

The first letter of the word 'astute' is '**a**'

The fifth letter of the word 'astute' is '**t**'

The sixth letter of the word 'astute' is '**e**'

So the answer is '**ate**'.

Mark the multiple choice answer box as shown

tea ☐
eat ☐
sat ☐
ate ▤
set ☐

'Words from Other Words 1' – Example Questions

In these questions, there are three pairs of words in brackets.
The second word, in each of the first two brackets, has been formed using some of the letters from the first word.
Find the missing word in the third bracket by using the same method as used in the first two brackets.
Mark the correct answer on your answer sheet.

Example   Answer

(piglet   pet)   (driven   den)   **ate**
         (astute   [?])

QUESTION 1

(ideal   idea)   (forte   fort)
         (realm   [?])

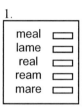

1.
- meal ⬚
- lame ⬚
- real ⬚
- ream ⬚
- mare ⬚

QUESTION 2

(bland   band)   (bloat   boat)
         (black   [?])

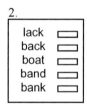

2.
- lack ⬚
- back ⬚
- boat ⬚
- band ⬚
- bank ⬚

QUESTION 3

(record   core)   (depart   pare)
         (ordeal   [?])

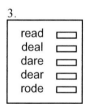

3.
- read ⬚
- deal ⬚
- dare ⬚
- dear ⬚
- rode ⬚

QUESTION 4

(spill   lisp)   (shard   dash)
         (stigma   [?])

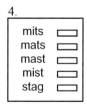

4.
- mits ⬚
- mats ⬚
- mast ⬚
- mist ⬚
- stag ⬚

QUESTION 5

(helper   peel)   (father   heat)
         (prefix   [?])

5.
- heat ⬚
- peel ⬚
- fixer ⬚
- fire ⬚
- reap ⬚

QUESTION 6

(damage   made)   (pirate   ripe)
      (racket   [?])

6.
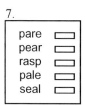

cart
tack
care
rack
rate

QUESTION 7

(relevant   veer)   (relative   tear)
      (relapse   [?])

7.
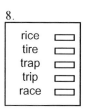

pare
pear
rasp
pale
seal

QUESTION 8

(levitate   teal)   (landfill   fail)
      (practice   [?])

8.
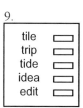

rice
tire
trap
trip
race

QUESTION 9

(trap   part)   (dial   laid)
      (edit   [?])

9.

tile
trip
tide
idea
edit

QUESTION 10

(catastrophe   cat)   (eagerly   eel)
      (police   [?])

10.

lice
lie
pie
pit
ice

QUESTION 11

(career   race)   (tabard   data)
      (lament   [?])

11.
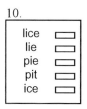

tale
meal
male
lean
team

QUESTION 12

(fearless   reel)   (sudden   dune)
      (ridden   [?])

12.
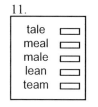

dire
dine
rend
rind
ride

What do they look like?...

In these questions, the middle word of each group has been made using some of the letters from the outer two words. The three words in the second group should go together in the same way as the three in the first group.
Find the word that is missing for the second group and mark it on your answer sheet.

(table [tub] supper)
(days [?   ] trick)

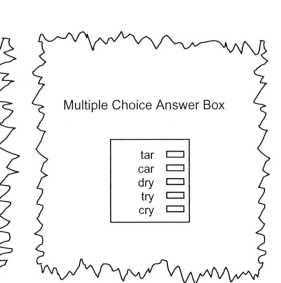

Multiple Choice Answer Box

tar ☐
car ☐
dry ☐
try ☐
cry ☐

How to set about answering them...

In these questions you need to make a new word for the second group by following the method that was used to make the middle word of the first group.

You first need to find out where the 't' of 'tub' came from. It came from the first letter of 'table'. Now, drop down to the lower line and take the first letter of 'days' so that you are using the same method.

Write 'd' in your empty bracket and continue to the second letter:

The 'u' of 'tub' came from the second letter of 'supper', therefore take the second letter of 'trick' in the lower line. Write this after the 'd' that you found. You now have 'dr' in your lower, middle bracket.

Finally, the 'b' of tub came from the third letter of 'table', therefore take the third letter of 'days' in the lower line.

By using the same method for the lower line as was used for the upper line, you will arrive at the word 'dry'.

Tips...

A letter used in the middle word within a bracket, may have been used more than once in the first word or second word or maybe both. Write down both letters and see which of the possible letter combinations fits with a word from the answer sheet.

Put an arrow alongside each letter position number that you write down to show whether the word that uses that letter, is to the right or the left of the middle word.

The Question......

(etch [late] alter)
(trip [?] actor)

The Answer Box......

cart	☐
part	☐
trip	☐
tort	☐
port	☐

STEP 1

Look at the centre word in the top bracket ('**late**') and then, taking each letter in turn, make a note of where else that letter appears in the words to the left and right of it.

The **first letter** ('**l**') appears only as the **second** letter of the word '**alter**'. Therefore, we need to take the **second** letter of the word '**actor**' ('**c**') on the line below and use this as the **first** letter of our answer.

The **second letter** ('**a**') appears only as the first letter of the word '**alter**'. Therefore, we need to take the **first** letter of the word '**actor**' ('**a**') and use this as the **second** letter of our answer.

The **third letter** ('**t**') appears in two places, firstly as the **second** letter of the word '**etch**' and secondly as the **third** letter of the word '**alter**'. Therefore, we need to take the **second** letter of the word '**trip**' ('**r**') and the **third** letter of the word '**actor**' ('**t**') and position them so that either could be used as the **third** letter of our answer.

The **fourth letter** ('**e**') appears in two places, firstly as the **first** letter of the word '**etch**' and secondly as the **fourth** letter of the word '**alter**'. Therefore, we need to take the **first** letter of the word '**trip**' ('**t**') and the **fourth** letter of the word '**actor**' ('**o**') and position them so that either could be used as the **fourth** letter of our answer.

STEP 2

The missing word must therefore be one of the following:- '**cart**', '**caro**', '**catt**' or **cato**'. The only properly spelt word is '**cart**' and the multiple choice answer sheet only provides '**cart**' as one of the options.

So the answer is '**cart**'.

Mark the multiple choice answer box as shown:

cart	▭
part	☐
trip	☐
tort	☐
port	☐

In these questions, the middle word of each group has been made using some of the letters from the outer two words.

The three words in the second group should go together in the same way as the three in the first group.

Find the word that is missing for the second group and mark it on your answer sheet.

Example   Answer

(grow [dog] sad)   **cat**
(trap [?] lock)

QUESTION 1

(model [nomad] train)
(alert [?] shrug)

1.
share	☐
shale	☐
grate	☐
great	☐
glare	☐

QUESTION 2

(touch [cadet] drake)
(llama [?] drone)

2.
dream	☐
drama	☐
model	☐
modem	☐
ladle	☐

QUESTION 3

(ruler [clear] chant)
(ethos [?] panda)

3.
paths	☐
phone	☐
those	☐
stand	☐
phase	☐

QUESTION 4

(tirade [crate] scout)
(coolers [?] appeal)

4.
polar	☐
poles	☐
poled	☐
polls	☐
poach	☐

QUESTION 5

(suite [virus] swerve)
(acidic [?] essence)

5.
sense	☐
nines	☐
dense	☐
niece	☐
nicer	☐

QUESTION 6

(staple [patch] chair)
(trifle [?] storm)

6.

flirt	☐
files	☐
first	☐
forms	☐
field	☐

QUESTION 7

(tuner [mitre] simple)
(lacrosse [?] pipette)

7.

piper	☐
pilot	☐
trail	☐
plate	☐
cross	☐

QUESTION 8

(foetus [comet] clamp)
(beset [?] gales)

8.

steer	☐
store	☐
frost	☐
forge	☐
geese	☐

QUESTION 9

(crown [cello] legal)
(gated [?] argue)

9.

great	☐
grate	☐
guard	☐
tread	☐
rated	☐

QUESTION 10

(status [album] marble)
(cache [?] refract)

10.

cared	☐
earth	☐
carat	☐
eater	☐
carer	☐

QUESTION 11

(stream [match] aching)
(adaptor [?] rerun)

11.

other	☐
order	☐
adept	☐
ordeal	☐
orbit	☐

QUESTION 12

(stain [spine] prose)
(banner [?] obtuse)

12.

beast	☐
brunt	☐
bones	☐
brute	☐
boats	☐

'Careful Reading and Thinking'

What do they look like?...

Alice, John, Alex, Sebrina and Mark all leave their homes at 8:15 a.m. to walk to school. Alex, who takes twice as long as Mark and half as long as Sebrina to get to school, arrives at 8:35. Alice and John both arrive at school ten minutes before Sebrina. Who arrives at school first ?

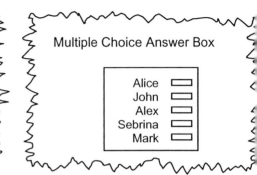

Multiple Choice Answer Box

Alice ☐
John ☐
Alex ☐
Sebrina ☐
Mark ☐

How to set about answering them...

These questions are all very different but, in general, they can be divided into three types:-

1) Those that require a **chart** to capture the information.

2) Those that are most readily worked out using a **diagram**.

3) Those that require a **timetable** to be drawn up. Being able to quickly identify which type of question you are looking at, will help you to work quickly towards the answer.

Each type will contain at least one 'key statement'. This is the definite piece of information given to you, such as 'Fred has five marbles'. Identifying the key statement is essential for answering these types of questions. Below each type is discussed in turn and, in the following pages, each type is examined with a worked example, followed up with two examples for you to try:-

1) Charts

You will be able to identify these types of questions as you will be given various pieces of information about things, such as people and their respective likes, dislikes, belongings etc.

It is necessary to read and to work through the information given and a clear chart will help you to find the answer here.

Draw the outline of your chart first and then plot the information as you read through the question. Remember that the clearer you make your chart, the less likely you are to make careless mistakes.

2) Diagrams

You will be able to identify these types of question as you will be given information about just one particular thing, such as the heights or ages of a group of people or maybe how many sweets or marbles they own.

By starting with the key statement (e.g. 'Fred has five marbles') you can then build a simple diagram from the other information provided (e.g. 'Terry has twice as many marbles as Fred').

By applying the other pieces of information to the diagram, you will be able to build a complete picture of the heights, ages or numbers of sweets or marbles owned.

There will always be a best place to start with these questions – this is often provided by the 'key statement'.

3) Timetables

You will be able to identify these as you are usually given details of some start times, arrival times and probably some travel times.

Again, you will always be given at least one definite piece of information and this is where you should begin.

Draw up your timetable grid and then start to populate it with the definite pieces of information e.g. 'Jane leaves home at 08:00'.

You will be able to fill in the rest of your timetable now by continuing to read carefully through the question whilst doing some simple workings.

When you have filled in as much of the given information as possible and completed all of the necessary workings, you will be able to use your timetable to find the answer.

Remember that the clearer you make your timetable, the less likely you are to make careless mistakes.

'Careful Reading and Thinking'
'Charts' – Worked Example

The Question……

The Answer Box……

Five friends stop at an ice cream parlour and each buys their favourite mix of flavours. Duncan picks strawberry, vanilla and chocolate. Hayes picks banana, vanilla and raspberry. Fred picks strawberry, raspberry and peach. Geoff picks banana and vanilla. Gary has the same as Hayes except that he has strawberry instead of banana.
Which of the following statements is true ?

A   Only Hayes has banana flavour.
B   Hayes, Geoff and Gary all have banana flavour.
C   Duncan, Fred and Gary all have strawberry flavour.
D   Everyone has vanilla flavour.
E   No one has chocolate flavour.

STEP 1

Read through the question and the five statements very carefully.

STEP 2

Build a chart and plot the information contained in the question as below:-

	Duncan	Hayes	Fred	Geoff	Gary
Strawberry	✓		✓		✓
Vanilla	✓	✓		✓	✓
Chocolate	✓				
Banana		✓		✓	
Raspberry		✓	✓		✓
Peach			✓		

STEP 3

Now read through the five statements again.

By using the chart you have made and reading the five statements very carefully, you can eliminate statements 'A', 'B', 'D' & 'E'. You are able to see that statement 'C' ('Duncan, Fred and Gary all have strawberry flavour ice cream.') is the only correct one.

So the answer is **C**.

Mark the multiple choice answer box as shown:

QUESTION 1

Oceanic Electronics make Sat Navs. There are 4 models in the range, the 'Hiker', the 'Explorer', the 'Pioneer' and the 'Adventurer'. The 'Hiker' model is waterproof and can play MP3 files. The 'Explorer' model is waterproof, has a touch screen and plays MP3 files. The 'Adventurer' model has a touch screen, 3D street view and European Maps.
The 'Pioneer' model has European Maps, a touch screen and is able to play MP3 files. Which of the following statements is true ?

A   Only the Explorer and Pioneer are able to play MP3 files.
B   The Hiker, Pioneer and Explorer all have touch screens.
C   The Adventurer and Hiker have European maps.
D   Only the Hiker and Explorer are waterproof.
E   The Adventurer is the only model without 3D street view.

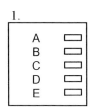

QUESTION 2

Julia and her friends talk about the books and magazines they enjoy reading.
Julia likes to always have a library book. She also likes to read the school magazine and her riding club magazine. Victoria also reads the riding club magazine but she enjoys a music magazine and the book club magazine too. Emily reads a music magazine, the school magazine and she likes to always have a library book. Sophie has the same as Victoria but she also reads the school magazine. Madeleine reads the same as Julia except she doesn't read the riding club magazine. How many of the friends read the riding club magazine?

A   5
B   4
C   3
D   2
E   1

2.

A ☐
B ☐
C ☐
D ☐
E ☐

The Question......

The Answer Box......

Terry, Ross, Adam, Henry and Edward each have a bag full of marbles.
Terry has ten more than Henry but five less than Adam.
Edward has twice as many marbles as Henry and three less than Ross.
If Terry has 16 marbles, which of the following statements is true ?

A   Terry has the most marbles.
B   Ross has less marbles than Terry.
C   Adam has nine marbles.
D   Henry has twenty six marbles.
E   Edward has the least marbles.

STEP 1

Read through the question and the five statements very carefully.

Jot down notes. Do not try to do this kind of question in your head.

STEP 2

Begin with the definite piece of information you are given – 'Terry has 16 marbles' – and set your notes out like this so that you can calculate how many marbles each of the others have by using each of the other pieces of information provided in the question:-

Terry = 16 marbles
Henry = 6 marbles   ('Terry has ten more than Henry....')
Adam = 21 marbles   ('Terry has.... but five less than Adam')
Edward = 12 marbles   ('Edward has twice as many marbles as Henry....')
Ross = 15 marbles   ('Edward has.....and three less than Ross')

STEP 3

Now read through the five statements again.

Put a cross against those which cannot be true. You can see that Ross has less marbles than Terry.

So the answer is **B**.

Mark the multiple choice answer box as shown:

QUESTION 1

Kiran is four years older than William was one year ago.
Alex is twice as old as Charlie.
If Callum was ten years old one year ago and he is now two years older than William, how old is Kiran ?

A   10
B   12
C   13
D   9
E   14

1.
A ▭
B ▭
C ▭
D ▭
E ▭

QUESTION 2

Anna has twice as many riding rosettes as Eleanor.
Lottie has four less riding rosettes than Anna.
Millie has twice as many riding rosettes as Lottie and half as many as Bella.
If Bella has twenty four riding rosettes, how many riding rosettes does Anna have ?

A   5
B   4
C   10
D   12
E   8

2.
A ▭
B ▭
C ▭
D ▭
E ▭

The Question......   The Answer Box......

Alice, John, Alex, Sebrina and Mark all leave their homes at 8:15 a.m. to walk to school. Alex, who takes twice as long as Mark and half as long as Sebrina to get to school, arrives at 8:35. Alice and John both arrive at school ten minutes before Sebrina. Who arrives at school first ?

A   Alice
B   John
C   Alex
D   Sebrina
E   Mark

STEP 1

Read through the question and the answer options very carefully.

STEP 2

Set out a timetable as below. This helps you to see the information very clearly. Begin with the definite information you have been given which is that Alex arrives at school at 08:35. Now, using the other information in the question, you can populate the rest of the timetable.

	Alice	John	Alex	Sebrina	Mark
Leave Home	08:15	08:15	08:15	08:15	08:15
Journey Time			20	40	10
Time of Arrival	08:45	08:45	08:35	08:55	08:25

It can be seen from the timetable that Mark arrives at school first.

So the answer is **E**.

 Mark the multiple choice answer box as shown:

QUESTION 1

'Bus A' left the bus terminal at 09:10 and arrived at its destination at 09:25. 'Bus B', which was held up in traffic and took an additional five minutes to complete the same journey, arrived at the destination at 09:35. At what time did 'Bus B' leave the bus terminal ?

A   09:10
B   09:40
C   09:25
D   09:35
E   09:15

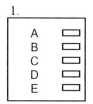

QUESTION 2

Alan and Joanna both had to travel from London to Newcastle for a 2.00 p.m. meeting.
Alan decided to take the train which normally takes 3 hours to complete the journey.
Joanna decided to drive even though the journey by car normally takes 5 hours.
Alan's train left London at 10.00 a.m. as planned but it broke down half way through the journey forcing Alan to wait half an hour for the next train to Newcastle.
Joanna arrived at the meeting 10 minutes before Alan.
Her journey had taken 5 hours as she had hoped. At what time did Joanna leave home ?

A   09:20
B   09:40
C   08:20
D   08:40
E   08:30

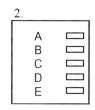

'Move a Letter'

1	L	5	I	9	S
2	E (the 2nd 'E')	6	R	10	I
3	L	7	O	11	T
4	R	8	N	12	V

'Missing Letter'

1	B	5	E	9	D
2	A	6	R	10	P
3	D	7	P	11	S
4	G	8	L	12	T

'Closest in Meaning'

1	likeable, popular	5	suppress, subdue	9	assessment, evaluation
2	tune, melody	6	rule, govern	10	curiosity, interest
3	favourite, preferred	7	edge, periphery	11	injury, wound
4	tranquil, calm	8	revolve, turn	12	enchanting, captivating

'Missing Three-Letter Word'

1	ONE	5	ALL	9	RED
2	CAP	6	ADD	10	PIE
3	LET	7	EAT	11	MEW
4	OWE	8	COG	12	FOR

'Word Associations'

1	road, track	5	loose, taut	9	propel, steer
2	weight, volume	6	find, found	10	France, Japan
3	trams, madam	7	slid, ran	11	hundred, ten
4	subtract, add	8	inwards, outwards	12	low, high

'Opposite in Meaning'

1	fast, slow	5	vast, minute	9	admire, detest
2	wealth, poverty	6	extend, shorten	10	generous, miserly
3	sturdy, rickety	7	thrilling, boring	11	gradual, abrupt
4	float, sink	8	victory, defeat	12	fair, unjust

Answers 2

'Hidden Four-Letter Word'

1	in church	5	in charge	9	see daylight
2	wide angle	6	paid less	10	Philip earned
3	panda really	7	garden table	11	new shirt
4	left his	8	drove round	12	noodles slowly

'Odd Two Out'

1	petal, stem	5	squirrel, end	9	bye, farewell
2	tools, garden	6	brake, leg	10	hang, picture
3	miniscule, size	7	quite, noise	11	fruit, orange
4	ruler, geometry	8	coach, plain	12	army, soldier

'Compound Words'

1	be have	5	ant elope	9	mess age
2	car rot	6	do main	10	off end
3	dam age	7	garb led	11	pad dock
4	an gel	8	ham mock	12	men ace

'Words with More than One Meaning'

1	rose	5	calf	9	rear
2	beat	6	felt	10	rest
3	tack	7	point	11	appeal
4	tap	8	ray	12	present

'Complete the Sum'

1	11	5	10	9	19
2	1	6	4	10	10
3	2	7	32	11	16
4	2	8	17	12	2

'Letters for Numbers'

1	B	5	C	9	A
2	B	6	C	10	D
3	D	7	B	11	E
4	E	8	D	12	B

Answers 3

'Number Patterns'

1	18	5	9	9	15
2	32	6	2	10	38
3	31	7	18	11	144
4	10	8	38	12	45

'Missing Number'

1	11	5	3	9	10
2	9	6	9	10	30
3	4	7	36	11	20
4	42	8	25	12	23

'Word Codes 1'

1	EPHT	5	VILPW	9	TNLYJ
2	LOCK	6	FLUSH	10	POISE
3	CKBBL	7	QMRJY	11	TFWBZ
4	SHRUB	8	TOOTH	12	ABBEY

'Word Codes 2'

1	REAL	5	SOUP	9	3217
2	5146	6	TOES	10	2521
3	5461	7	MOAT	11	SPIN
4	2167	8	6523	12	PIES

'Alphabet Codes'

1	FI	5	KB	9	DW
2	GH	6	FC	10	AD
3	IN	7	XW	11	UL
4	WB	8	LQ	12	MI

'Letter Patterns'

1	IS	5	QJ	9	PK
2	IH	6	YF	10	IZ
3	VF	7	FS	11	RD
4	UO	8	CW	12	NW

'Words from Other Words 1'

1	real	5	fire	9	tide
2	back	6	cart	10	pie
3	dear	7	pear	11	tale
4	mist	8	trip	12	dine

'Words from Other Words 2'

1	glare	5	niece	9	great
2	model	6	first	10	carer
3	phone	7	pilot	11	order
4	polar	8	geese	12	bones

'Careful Reading and Thinking'

'Charts'		'Diagrams'		'Timetables'	
1	D	1	B	1	E
2	C	2	C	2	C